The Yarn Palette

The Yarn Palette

The Ultimate Visual Guide to Choosing the Right
Colour, Texture & Style for Every Pattern

Claire Montgomerie

First published in 2008

A QUINTET BOOK

Published by A&C Black
38 Soho Square
London W1D 3HB

www.acblack.com

ISBN: 978-1408-101-339

This book was designed and produced by
Quintet Publishing Limited,
6 Blundell Street, London N7 9BH, UK

Senior Project Editor: Katy Bevan
Designer: Bonnie Bryan
Photographer: Sian Irvine
Art Director: Sofia Henry
Managing Editor: Donna Gregory

QTT.KYA

Manufactured in Singapore by Pica Digital Pte
Printed in China by SNP Leefung Printers Ltd

10 9 8 7 6 5 4 3 2 1

Contents

Introduction

Each of us has a unique understanding of colour – and different preferences for the many various shades and tints. I have a passion for the glorious colour palettes associated with the landscapes, environments and objects that surround us. *Knitter's Yarn Palette* aims to help knitters trust their intuition when using these inspirations to create beautiful knitted designs.

For knitwear designers the depth and variety of yarn shades is breathtaking, and this book showcases a wide range and demonstrates how to use them successfully.

While working in a yarn shop, I witnessed the mesmerizing effect a rainbow of yarn can have on a customer's senses. I indulged my own obsession by walking slowly past the multicoloured boxes of delicately dyed skeins and drinking in the hues while sneaking a touch of the tactile fibres. I cannot leave a yarn shop without taking away a little bit of that sensory explosion to remind me of any ideas that formed. This usually means, like most knitters, I end up with a large collection of odd balls of yarn in all colours, textures and fibres.

The problem for most yarn hoarders is that they are unsure of what to do with all these pretty bundles. I use mine to embroider – as edgings and complementary textures – but mainly for inspiration.

Looking at the quality of one twist of yarn, or a couple of skeins of contrasting yarns in dreamy shades, is enough to spark a few design ideas. However, most knitters are nervous about acting on this innate love of yarn and colour, fearing they are not creative enough or won't live up to the fantastic potential.

Many knitters will not stray from the pattern's instructions for fear of ruining the final product. This leads to a process that is not necessarily artistic, and therefore ultimately unsatisfying – especially for an accomplished knitter. *Knitter's Yarn Palette* encourages you to experiment, and displays alternative colour swatches, designs and yarn substitutions.

Our objective is to provide an inspirational guide to knitting innovatively, proving that you do not need an art-school education to be creative. Although experienced knitters may feel confident with experimentation, beginners can also be innovative. Plain scarves or throws are the perfect blank canvas to start your creative knitting because of their simple construction. Since there is no need for a perfect fit, you can choose from a wide range of yarn and stitches.

Page by page, *Knitter's Yarn Palette* will inform and inspire, guiding you through the creative process. Its wealth of stunning photography and its invaluable yarn archive will serve as useful reference points for many stunning projects.

– Claire Montgomerie

How to use this book

This book is divided into three main sections: Yarn and Colour, The Colour Palettes, and the Yarn Directory.

Colour and yarn

The first section deals with finding sources of inspiration, using what you find, turning ideas into beautiful designs, and then choosing the colours, fibres and structures. Here is where you will discover all you need to know to begin experimenting – from the basics, such as choosing an alternative yarn from your colour palette for a pattern, to selecting the colours for a stripe sequence or creating a new knitted stitch to complement your yarn selection.

The projects

These are arranged into six separate chapters, or themes, to highlight the diversity of the designs and colour palettes that can be achieved from different research.
The first theme is **Into the Blue**,

Beautiful, inspirational photographs of landscapes are included. Each image showcases yarns that work in that palette.

For each chapter, we've compiled a mood board to demonstrate the various choices of material to consider when compiling your yarn palette.

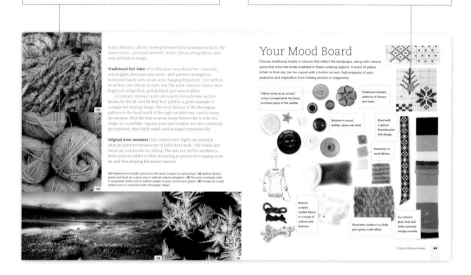

an ocean- and beach-inspired chapter that shows the whole range of ocean colours, from the cool, faded, temperate beach palettes to the rich, deep brights of the tropical seas.
 Frozen Monochrome derives from research into an arctic climate, evocative of

sparkling ice and snow and a mainly white, grey and ice-blue palette, demonstrating how even neutral colours can inspire beautiful knitwear designs.
 Enchanted Woodland is reminiscent of the woods, earth and leaves of late summer to autumn. The palette uses

understated, natural colours – mossy greens with a hint of brown, fawn and rust.

Fourth in this section is **Tropical Storm,** which reflects the vibrant colours and textures of the rainforest.

Country Pastels is a palette inspired by the countryside, the spring and wildflowers, leading to a delicately soft-hued range of yarns and colours.

Finally, **Desert Sands** is based around the colours of barren, hot desert landscapes, in a warm, sunny palette of shimmering golds, oranges, reds and yellows.

All of the chapters include beautiful photographs of related scenes and yarns used in the research and design of the patterns. Use these as a springboard for your own designs.

The yarn directory

The Yarn Directory provides you with a list of some of the types of yarns used in the patterns and showcased throughout the book. The yarns are arranged by weight, making it simple to identify an appropriate substitute. Keep in mind, though, that you always need to make a swatch to check your tension.

> Each project is illustrated with close-up pictures of the finished item.

> Full patterns for each project are given, with clear charts where they are needed.

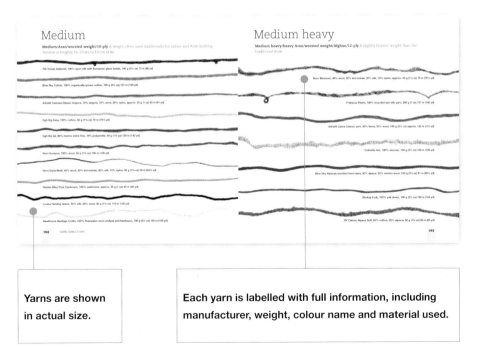

> Yarns are shown in actual size.

> Each yarn is labelled with full information, including manufacturer, weight, colour name and material used.

Yarn and colour

Fibre sources, spinning,
understanding colour and dyes

The Creative Process

Before you start an experimental knitting project, you need to think about your creative process. Many knitters are extremely logical, due to the mathematical and rhythmic nature of knitting. This sometimes leads to the belief that there is no room for creativity in their designs, because an 'artistic' work method is often seen as random and whimsical.

Organized chaos

In fact, most designers plan their projects meticulously so the final creation will work both aesthetically and practically. The artistry comes from the initial inspiration and in the way you develop this idea and apply it to the final fabric.

Keep your ball bands – they contain valuable information.

Creative toolbox

Every designer needs a sketchbook of some kind to capture her ideas, whether it is a detailed journal of inspirational surroundings, a collaged mood board, a photograph album, a colour documentation or a simple notebook. However, you don't need to worry about your drawing skills, chaotic handwriting or computer literacy. An album of holiday photos or a collection of souvenirs from trips or special occasions can be fantastic springboards for creativity. If you find something interesting, evocative or beautiful – perhaps while on holiday, a nature walk or even a shopping trip – note it down, take a picture, or if possible, take it with you.

A digital camera is a perfect tool to document your inspirational finds. You can take as many shots of your subject as you wish, and delete the boring, blurred or poorly lit ones without the expense of processing.

Once these initial evocative sketches, photos or inspiring paraphernalia have been compiled, it is simply a matter of working out the best way to express the inspiration – literally or symbolically. At this stage it is a good idea to consider your studies closely, drawing on the particular shapes, textures and colours you find interesting. Isolate these features and concentrate on them. If you are

Mood boards help arrange your thoughts visually.

using particular objects or themes with a cultural significance, consider researching the historical context to uncover any appealing craft techniques, fibres or hues that may be relevant to your project.

Expressive stitches

Knitting and manipulating fabric are both techniques that can accurately represent physical textures, shapes and colours in multiple ways. Knitting can be worked two- or three-dimensionally in myriad complex or simple stitches, shapes and fibres.

A stitch dictionary is an invaluable tool at this point. It would be impossible for a knitted textile designer to remember every stitch ever invented over many centuries; therefore it isn't cheating if you use techniques from these compilations in your projects.

If it is an ambience, emotion or memory you wish to evoke, your task can be much harder. Colour is a great way to suggest mood. Most people link certain colours to particular thoughts and feelings. For instance, red can symbolize danger or excitement, or romantic love and passion.

Other methods include using yarn and fibre in experimental and original ways or integrating elements of the initial inspiration in your work, such as making beads from pebbles or wood that you have gathered.

Finished shapes

The final step is to create the finished product. This involves making sketches and patterns to follow when making the project. Do not worry if you are not a great artist, the sketches do not have to be perfect, but they do need very clear measurements, so a tape measure is a must.

It's also a good idea to look at garment shapes in shops for inspiration. If you are using a theme with a cultural history, research the clothing shapes of that period. You can also use measurements and shapes from your own clothes as a guideline. If pattern writing seems too daunting, stick to the good old scarf, wrap or blanket, which do not require a difficult pattern. Just pick up some needles, cast on some stitches, be inspired by your mood boards and photographs, and play with the yarn and texture of the fabric until you reach the desired length. Then simply cast off. What could be easier?

If certain colours appear together in nature, chances are they will look good when you put them side by side as well.

Creating a Mood Board

When inspiration strikes, a mood board is a great tool for gathering your ideas in one place, so you can easily access all of your research and use it as a reference point.

Putting it together

The informality of this conceptual board means important aesthetic components of the theme can be put together before you choose yarn, or begin knitting. This allows you to decide which parts are important before executing the final design, and this saves time and reknitting later.

Compile images you may have documented in your sketchbook or in photographs, alongside pictures of scenes or garments that stimulate your creativity, collected from magazines or the Internet. Piece together odds and ends from places that aroused an interest, such as leaves, flowers, labels, train tickets and so on. You can include snippets of pattern and colour from wallpapers, fabrics or old clothes.

Choosing a colour palette

In fact, anything that relates to the research and final product can be displayed, but an essential, binding factor is the colour palette.

This reference, represented by splashes of paint, swatches of fabric or twists of yarn ensures that the final product stays true to the colours that inspired you from the start. Knit small swatches of possible stitch structures in relevant colours, and assess their viability in relation to the final design.

In spite of all of these components, a mood board does not need to take forever to assemble; it should be a quick representation of all of the possibilities for a clothing design – not a work of art. It must, however, be neat and easy to read so that it is easy to make your final pattern and colour choices.

Knit small swatches in new yarns or colourways: this is the same bouclé yarn used in the muff on page 56.

Try out colour combinations by wrapping yarn around a strip of cardboard.

Buttons can be used in your final project.

Tiny snippets of fabric or braid will help you collate textures, as well as a colour palette.

Seeds and leaves can be collected on walks.

Make small wraps of yarn and keep a record of the ball bands.

Sequoia mood board

This mood board was used to inspire the Sequoia Shawl (in the Enchanted Woodland palette, pages 74 to 79). The inspiration initially came from a felled tree stump in a wooded area. To echo the exposed rings on the stump, the designer chose to construct a semi-circular shawl composed of stripes in woody colours. But to capture the forest feel a mood board was needed.

The designer collected objects from the ground, and added yarns in autumn colours and some bouclé yarn that provides a great texture. Its loops and whorls are reminiscent of the rings on the tree stump, as well as dappled light filtering in through foliage. Extra yarn was threaded around the rows to emphasize the rings. The final project creates a feel of mosses, leaves, trees and light.

Understanding Colour

Colour theory is an incredibly complex subject, mainly because many of the judgements can be subjective; how many times have you discussed whether a particular colour is red or orange, green or turquoise? This section is an overview of the basics – you don't need to know everything about colour to make aesthetic decisions such as selecting yarn to stripe with a blue tone.

Use yarns you love

Most of these opinions are intuitive and personal. However, a little knowledge will give you some insight as to which colours to place together when choosing yarns. And you may discover combinations and contrasts that you had not thought of before. Always remember that colour perceptions are essentially personal. In other words, always knit with colours that, first and foremost, you love – you may feel stuck looking at them as you knit for days, weeks or even months.

The technical part

Essentially, colour is the result of the absorption and reflection of light as observed by the eye and processed by the brain.

There are seven wavelengths in light; each of these is a colour. The most obvious way to see this effect is in a rainbow, which occurs when sunlight passes through raindrops, acting as a prism, that creates this spectrum of colours.

The colour spectrum

When light hits an object – as opposed to a prism – the light is absorbed or reflected in different ways, depending on its material composition. As a rule, light colours reflect more

A rainbow shows the whole spectrum of colour.

Colour and texture are intimately entwined in yarns.

light than they absorb, and dark colours have the opposite effect. The way in which the human eye channels the light and the brain processes it is unique to each person. This is why the perception of colours, shades and tints is so personal.

Environmental factors

A colour is also affected by its environment. An object's perceived hue can vary greatly when placed next to articles of different shades or tints. This is where a colour wheel can help. It is essentially a representation of the colours in the spectrum and their relationship to each other, which is useful when choosing a yarn palette for a project. Using a colour wheel can help you successfully put colours together.

Seasonal changes

The seasons affect quality and intensity of light. These factors can be useful when choosing colours to reflect certain themes and moods. Cool colours are often chosen for an overcast, or stormy landscape, and warm hues for a sunny day.

Keep in mind that the amount of light the yarn fibre absorbs or reflects will alter its colour intensity. In fact, in some lights, shiny fibres like silk will change colour completely. However, this can be harnessed to complement some themes that call for iridescent hues and movement.

The Colour Wheel

Each colour has its own contextual history and psychology, which is defined by individual cultural and personal influences. This can also help you choose shades to echo a theme.

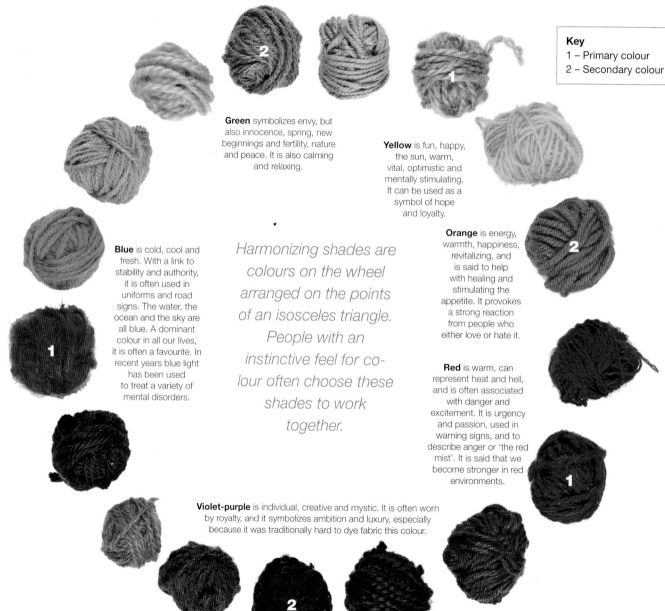

Key
1 – Primary colour
2 – Secondary colour

Green symbolizes envy, but also innocence, spring, new beginnings and fertility, nature and peace. It is also calming and relaxing.

Yellow is fun, happy, the sun, warm, vital, optimistic and mentally stimulating. It can be used as a symbol of hope and loyalty.

Blue is cold, cool and fresh. With a link to stability and authority, it is often used in uniforms and road signs. The water, the ocean and the sky are all blue. A dominant colour in all our lives, it is often a favourite. In recent years blue light has been used to treat a variety of mental disorders.

Orange is energy, warmth, happiness, revitalizing, and is said to help with healing and stimulating the appetite. It provokes a strong reaction from people who either love or hate it.

Red is warm, can represent heat and hell, and is often associated with danger and excitement. It is urgency and passion, used in warning signs, and to describe anger or 'the red mist'. It is said that we become stronger in red environments.

Harmonizing shades are colours on the wheel arranged on the points of an isosceles triangle. People with an instinctive feel for colour often choose these shades to work together.

Violet-purple is individual, creative and mystic. It is often worn by royalty, and it symbolizes ambition and luxury, especially because it was traditionally hard to dye fabric this colour.

Primary colours

A good place to start on the colour wheel is with the primary colours – red, yellow and blue – which cannot be produced by mixing other colours together. These form the points of a triangle on the wheel. All of the other colours come in between these, and they are formed by mixing the colours on either side of them.

The next group is composed of the secondary colours, which are made by mixing equal amounts of the two primaries on either side of them on the wheel: These are orange (red and yellow), green (yellow and blue) and violet (blue and red).

The tertiary colours are mixtures of a primary and secondary colour. These are red-orange, red-violet, blue-green, blue-violet, yellow-green and yellow-orange. This creates 12 colours in the wheel. There are of course infinitely more hues, shades and tints in between.

Simultaneous contrast

Complementary colours are placed opposite each other on a colour wheel. These colours differ the most from one another, and therefore provide the greatest contrast. This process is also known as simultaneous contrast. A colour appears more brilliant when it is surrounded by its complement. Think of a green landscape and how that green seems even lusher, and more vibrant when a boy wearing a red sweater walks across it. This is a technique often used by painters like John Constable, for instance, in his famous painting *The Hay Wain*.

Blue or cool colours may appear to recede, and red or warm colours advance when placed next to each other. This can be important in stripes, and should be considered when choosing yarns, depending on which colours you want to be more dominant or submissive, or when you want an optical effect of movement.

Neutral colours

Achromatic colours are those that lack strong colour; black, white and most greys fit this group, and pastels, browns and tans are near neutrals. All of these can be used to offset a bright colour or colours and make them more wearable. However, remember that even these can affect the quality of shade; colour can appear lighter on a black background but it also increases its saturation or brightness, and on a white background the shade can appear darker, showing off all its hues equally. Neutrals take on a hue of the complementary colour to the shade they are next to – a grey stripe placed next to a red one will take on a greenish tint.

Tansy makes
yellow or green.

Marigold flowers
produce yellows.

Cochineal beetles
make a deep red, or
carmine, dye.

Alder buckthorn
creates browns
and yellow dyes.

Dyes and Nature

Natural dyes have been around almost as long as people have been making their own clothes. These dyes were derived from both animal and vegetable sources and boiled with the cloth to apply the colour. In the mid-nineteenth century the first synthetic dyes were developed. Now there is a huge variety of dyes for different fibres.

Naturally does it

Some fibres, such as silk and wool, take dyes easily, but most need a mordant in order to work. Mordants aid the reaction between the fibre and the dye so that the colour will 'take' and be colourfast. The fact that most plant, animal and synthetic fibres take dyes differently can be used to create interesting striations of colour.

Intense colours are achieved through hand dyeing.

There are a number of chemical dyes that are commonly used. However, the natural types are innumerable, and their pigmentation is often surprising. As the world becomes more ecologically aware, there is an increasing demand for natural dyes, and plantation crops for dyeing.

Natural dyes can be sorted into three types: animal, vegetable and mineral. All parts of a plant can usually be used: leaves, roots, stems, seeds and fruit. Most berries produce great shades, but they are not particularly colourfast. Plants generally provide unlimited variants of pale brown and green shades, with just a few providing fast and clear colours without any help. However, there are some plants that produce natural vibrant colours, and these were indispensable in ancient times.

Historic colours

Woad, a flowering plant, has produced blue dyes for centuries; as well as dyeing cloth the ancient Europeans used it to paint tattoos on their bodies. However, while wool produced beautiful shades, it was not so good with cellulose fibres. Indigo plants had to be used to obtain deeper blues.

Elderberries make a grey-purple dye.

Walnut husks dye a pale brown.

Elderberries can produce yellow, blue or black with different mordants (compounds used to set dyes).

The history of red dye can go back to textiles found in King Tutankhamun's Egyptian tomb that were dyed in madder—a red pigment was produced from the roots of the plant. Red-orange pigment came from henna, and a yellow was produced by boiling a whole weld plant.

A particularly tricky colour to dye in ancient times was purple. It was made from the secretions of the murex mollusk, which meant that very small quantities of pigment were extracted. Thousands were needed for one ounce of dye, making it very expensive. It became a popular, ostentatious choice of colour; the wealthy and royalty were the only people who could afford it. Purple is still associated with royalty today.

Around the fifteenth century, insect dyes became popular. In fact, cochineal from the *dactylopius coccus* beetle is still a popular red pigment today. Bark also produces strong, deep hues. Along with it came the saying "dyed-in-the-wood" or "dyed-in-the-wool" to describe people who were loyal through and through—both sayings derived from the strength of colour that was produced. Although bark produces very deep colouring, the pigments do not always provide the browns you might expect. Fustic, or pistachio tree bark, supplies yellow, and red maple is a source of

purple. Brazil wood dyes red, and logwood makes black dye. A deep red dye traditionally used in the Scottish highlands was obtained from lichen scraped from rocks and steeped in urine.

Mineral dyes come from inorganic materials. Limestone produces lime or white; ochre, a derivative of iron oxide, produces myriad yellows, oranges and reds; lead oxide creates red; and malachite contributes green.

Limestone is used as a pigment for limes and whites.

The flowering plant woad is used to make blue dyes.

Colour and mood

How the colour is dyed onto the yarn can influence the final effect. A yarn dyed with a small percentage of colour, or exposed to the dye for a short period of time will produce lighter colours – the longer a yarn is allowed to steep, the darker it becomes. These subtle differences in tone can be used to great effect, and even the same fibre with different intensities can be used to evoke the changing seasons.

Bark creates very deep brown colours.

Fibre Sources

Since the inception of making cloth, a wide variety of fibres have been used to spin yarn. In fact, some newfangled yarns are not as modern as you might think. Nettles, for example, have been used in clothing for thousands of years. The plant only lost favour because of the comparative ease of harvesting cotton. Nettles made a resurrection at the start of the twentieth century, when they were used in German military uniforms because the war reduced the availability of cotton and wool.

Animal, vegetable and mineral

The twenty-first century resurgence of natural fibres is partially due to concerns about the manufacturing processes used to make synthetic yarns. Nonetheless, natural and synthetic fibres have advantages and disadvantages, and both can be useful in experimental knitting.

Vegetable fibres are mostly comprised of cellulose, and they come from various parts of the plant. An excellent example is cotton, which is harvested from seed. Hemp, soybean and banana are collected from around the skin of the stem. And bamboo and linen are gathered from the stalk. Fibres can also be obtained from fruits, such as coconut, and its leaves, which is the case with sisal. Paper and bark yarns are derived from cellulose fibres, too.

Animal fibres contain proteins, which are usually from animal hair, such as wool, angora, cashmere, llama and even dog. From the silkworms' cocoons comes silk, another prominent animal fibre.

Mineral fibres include metals and fibreglass, which are occasionally used as embellishments.

The housewife's dream

Synthetic fibres were created to replicate or improve the qualities of natural fibres. This class includes nylon, polyester and acrylic. Man-made fibres such as rayon or viscose are manufactured but not completely synthetic, because they are produced from cellulose fibres. Rayon was

1 Yarns come from alpaca and camel. 2 A cashmere goat. 3 Plant cellulose creates strong fibre. 4 The llama family produces soft fibres. 5 Nettles are an ancient source of fabrics. 6 Coconut husks are good for more than string. 7 and 8 Silk cocoons in their raw state. 9 An angora rabbit. 10 Ripe cotton buds are picked laboriously by hand.

developed in the mid-nineteenth century as an artificial silk. Scientists have always been intrigued by the strength of silk, and some have researched the production of an artificial spider-silk fibre.

Acrylic was developed as a synthetic wool because it is popular for knitting, looks like wool, is lightweight, resilient, moth resistant, and is incredibly colourfast. However, it pills easily, is not as insulating as wool, and is not always as soft.

These new fabrics and fibres aimed to be the answer to every housewife's dream: incredibly crease-proof, simple to maintain, easily dyed and cheap to produce. However, the wearing qualities didn't always live up to the hype.

The best of both worlds

Perhaps the answer is to combine fibres to the best of both worlds. Some of the most durable and comfortable yarns today are a mixture of natural and synthetic fibres. Merino wool socks, for example, are luxurious, but they are likely to wear out.

Therefore, most sock yarns have a little nylon or another synthetic fibre added to the natural yarn to increase durability. Many yarns are now treated or mixed with synthetics, so they can be machine-washed without risk of felting. These synthetic fibres are all fabulous, but natural yarns still have their uses. There is no need to create water-repellent, insulating and light fibres when wool has all of these qualities. When wool is spun and knitted properly, it is naturally unsurpassed in all of these qualities.

Most natural fibres tend to have fantastic drape, which is an added benefit to their naturally practical qualities, such as the strength of silk. Synthetic yarns can be used well in fancy yarns to create unusual textures, such as eyelash fringing. Strange, knobbly yarns that do not shed hair or fibre can be good for allergy sufferers.

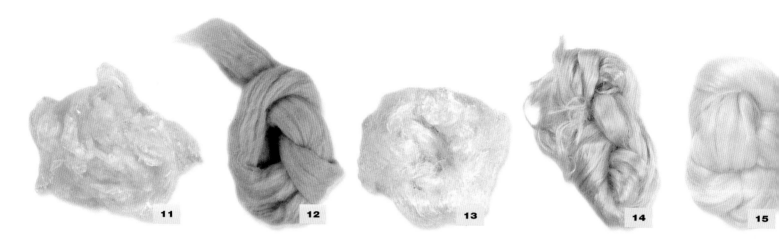

11 12 13 14 15

Fibre Structure

A fibre's qualities often dictates how it is used. Cotton yarn is usually spun with a smooth finish and it is durable, making it the traditional and best choice for crochet. It is available in a range of weights and colours, including many fabulous summer shades – it is often used as a summer-weight alternative to wool. Cotton usually has a matte finish. However, if you prefer cotton with a shine and extra strength, use mercerized cotton. Organic cotton is a sustainable alternative to plants grown with fertilizers and chemicals. And it is easy to reprocess – there are many varieties of recycled cotton yarn available.

Yarns galore

There are many varieties of wool and mohair, derived from sheep and goats. The qualities vary from merino to cashmere to kid mohair, but all of them are extremely warm and usually soft and matt.

Silk is incredibly strong, with a mesmerizing sheen and drape that adds to its luxury. This is a great summer choice and fabulous when mixed with matte yarns. Synthetic yarns can have a multitude of qualities, thicknesses and textures.

22

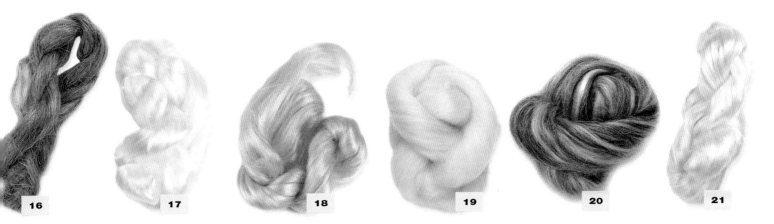

11 Silk-like and sustainable, unspun bamboo fibres. 12 Green untreated cotton. 13 Italian silk waste. 14 Soybean protein fibre – long filaments and a silky sheen. 15 Milk protein fibre from casein. 16 Flax or linen fibres. 17 Tencel or lyocell made from cellulose. 18 Tussah silk from wild silk worms. 19 Wool from the merino sheep. 20 Black alpaca mixed with silk fibres. 21 Mulberry silk from silk worms that eat only the leaves of the mulberry tree. 22 A low whorl, drop spindle is basic equipment for portable spinning. With a small amount of practice, the twisting of the fibres can create a beautiful handspun yarn.

When they are combined with natural yarns, they can help garments hold their shape when worn and washed.

Spinning yarns

All of these fibres can be spun into many types of yarn: they can be one long, smooth plied length or varied to create fancy yarns, such as bouclé, gimp, slub, eyelash and chenille. The yarn does not always need to be spun. It can be used in its essential form, as roving, or the fibre can be knitted into a tape yarn or woven into a ribbon yarn. All of these yarns have particular qualities that can be incorporated into your knitting to inspire and create themes. A ribbon can evoke draping fabric or tumbling water. A roving yarn retains the look of the fleece it was carded from, making fluffy sheeplike clouds in knitted fabrics.

And the drama of eyelash yarn, depending on its lengths, can represent the fringing, curling tendrils of plant stamens or lush coverings of moss.

All of these yarns are classified by weight, thickness or ply, so it is easy for the knitter to substitute yarns, select the correct needles and judge the right tension. The detailed summary of these classifications on pages 156 to 159 and list of yarns in the Yarn Directory at the back of the book will make it easier to choose alternative yarns for the patterns and can also be used as a guide when you choose yarns for your own projects.

Designing Fabrics

Knitters of all experience levels can benefit from experimenting with stitch, shape and structure. The basic knit-and-purl stitches make up most other techniques, so once these stitches are learned, they can be arranged in countless ways to create wonderful new fabrics. You can accomplish this by simply playing with the stitches, or if you are a little hesitant, by using a stitch manual to try out some of the many techniques that are available.

Record your experiments

Keep your references close at hand to compare the textures you create to the qualities you are trying to capture. You don't need to stick to just one technique or yarn; tension swatches are great tools for inserting as many methods, yarns and fibres into your work as possible. These small squares of knitting allow you to physically test the fibres and stitches that you feel will suit your theme – without knitting entire garments.

When you have knitted enough of these samples to satisfy your creativity and curiosity, it is time to select the most successful combinations, measure your tension, and move on to your pattern.

If you tend to knit numerous samples, keep notes in your reference sketchbooks to remember the needle size(s), yarn name, quality and shade numbers you used in each one. There is nothing more frustrating than making a beneficial mistake in a sample, and not remembering how to recapture that exact texture.

Taking measurements

When calculating your tension, make sure that you first block your swatch lightly. Next take a few measurements at different points in the swatch to get an average, because hand knitting is often uneven. You are looking for the number of stitches and rows per centimetre or inch.

Once this is determined, you can write a pattern for anything by using that particular stitch on the same size needle. It will be necessary to take tension measurements for each technique, needle change or yarn swap within the sample; if the tension is significantly different, it could greatly affect the size of the finished garment.

Always keep your references close at hand.

Keep the labels with your yarn so you can find them again.

Swatches from other, older projects may be useful in the future.

Sizing

Take as many body measurements as possible, especially when you design a fitted garment. Once you have the number of stitches knitted to one centimetre, or inch, all the measurements can be converted to stitches with simple maths. For example, multiply the measurement at the cast-on edge by the amount of stitches per centimetre to get the amount of stitches necessary to cast on.

The same simple maths is used for rows, although in this case, it may be easier to simply knit to the desired length. You will know the number of stitches you begin with at the start of shaping, the number you need to end up with, and the amount of rows there are to shape your knitted piece. So you can calculate the number of increases needed and the intervals at which they should be applied.

The Colour Palettes

From inspiration to live projects – the creative process in action

Into the blue

The ocean is a large place – around

70 per cent of the Earth is covered in water. The intense colours of corals and iridescent sea life are inspirational, while the main muse must be the water itself: its liquid movement and the intensity of its colours. The focal point of the theme is the seabed, seaweed and fish.

Watercolours

The challenge of creating the movement of tides and waves in knitting is achieved through the clever use of yarn, fibre and colour. Yarns that shimmer, are space-dyed (yarn which is dyed with several different colours for a multifaceted effect), dip-dyed, hand-painted, or use unusual dyeing techniques will change colour subtly along their length. Overlapping colours, speckles or the incorporation of different fibres in one yarn may cause the same dyes and colours to take differently.

The shine of a fibre will also affect the way in which the dye takes and colour reflects and may appear more intense and iridescent or even change its shade, depending on the light. Silks, viscose, rayon, some cotton fibres, and other man-made yarns can be shiny and

1 Fish shine with colour. **2** Silky yarns emulate the seabed. **3** Light and movement are reflected in the sea. **4** The ocean illuminates with exotic iridescent colour. **5** Colour and texture abound on the shore. **6** Movement and colour are captured in yarns and ribbons.

7

8

9

10

11

12

slinky in their drape when knitted – perfect for reproducing a fluid, watery movement in a finished project.

Consider how to use the yarn to its full effect. If you have a fantastically unusual yarn with a fabulous drape, then let it show – don't hide it in a tight stitch. Try a long fur stitch or dropped stitches to expose your yarn. Alternatively, you could apply the yarn after knitting by using it in long, dramatic tassels.

Shoreline

Colours on the shore are washed out and bleached by the sun; dusky blue skies peppered with grey; the sandy yellows of the beach and dunes; pale browns, greys and faded pinks of shells; wood and pebbles worn by the tides and the weather; bright whites and pastel shades of waterside abodes. Don't forget, too, the brightness provided by the cheery striped deckchairs and windbreaks. The seashore really does induce feelings of relaxation.

7 Capture the colours of the shore, shells and corals. **8** Smooth ridges in sandy shades reflect the shoreline. **9** Texture, light and shade add inspiration. **10** The power of the sea is visible on the beach. **11** Striped texture is inspired by shady sands. **12** Ropes and buoys are tangled like yarn. **13** Sky blue, reds and pinks in a late sunset. **14** Seaweed and coral colours are combined in a swatch. **15** Coral ribbing plays with light and shade. **16** Coiled skeins evoke the tangled nets and rusty chains on the shoreline.

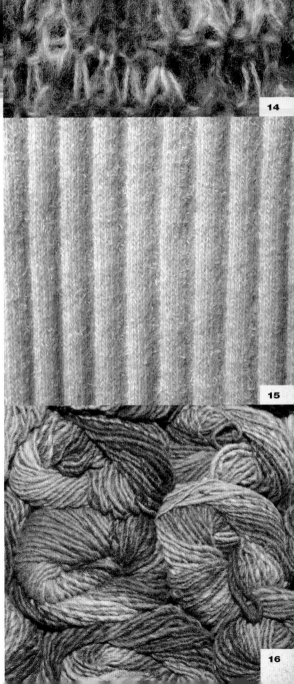

Shell collection Collect the washed-up treasure, the flotsam and jetsam found at the sea edge, as a way of documenting these colours and textures for future reference when researching yarns and techniques. For example, bits of old fishing net and string can easily be represented by knitting in pretty cottons or even with the string itself. The ridges on shells or sea-worn driftwood can be represented with garter ridges or ripple stitches. The debris can even be attached to the work itself, knitted in as you go, by threading shells with natural holes onto the yarn like beads, or sewn on top of the fabric after it is made.

Splashes of colour from brightly striped deckchairs, or formed by the painted wooden slats of waterside homes, can easily be interpreted into striped designs. The ripples of gentle waves with crescents of white foam and bubbles as they lap against the shore can be represented by soft foamy lace falling in ruffles and layers of pretty scalloped edgings. Even the beachwear you may once have worn can be reused, or its colours used as inspiration for new pieces.

17 Deckchair-like stripes bring in an element of holiday colour. **18** Braided ropes echo the shore, with rust stains amid fishing nets. **19** Shells, beads and stones can be dyed and painted and retain their texture.

Experiment

Using new or unusual materials is a good way to begin experimenting with textures. Here, natural raffia in the colours of the sand and the sea is reminiscent of beach hats and bags. Use different stitches to see the effect – try dropping stitches the length of your swatch. The run will stop when it reaches the cast-on row, creating a net of horizontal bars.

Your Mood Board

Seaside elements can be collected from the shore itself. Revisit your childhood by gathering shells on the beach. Also gather together ribbons, fabrics and yarns that evoke the elements of the ocean: the shells, seaweed and sand, as well as the dark blues and greens of the deep.

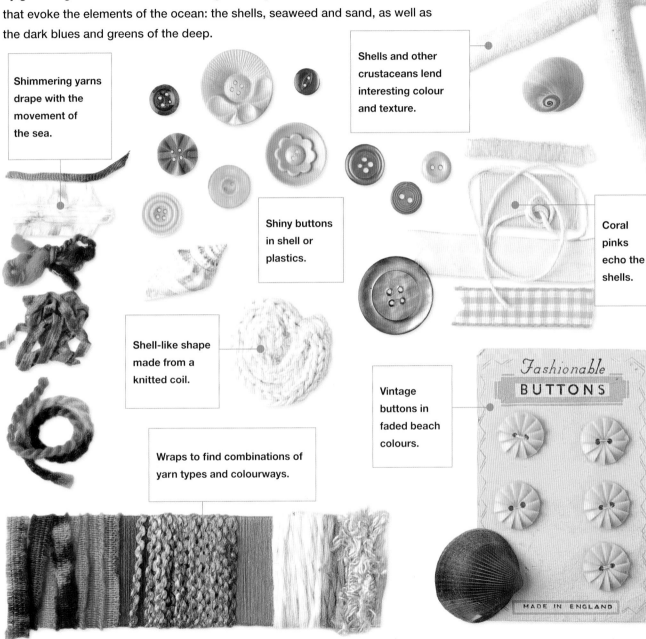

Shimmering yarns drape with the movement of the sea.

Shells and other crustaceans lend interesting colour and texture.

Shiny buttons in shell or plastics.

Coral pinks echo the shells.

Shell-like shape made from a knitted coil.

Vintage buttons in faded beach colours.

Wraps to find combinations of yarn types and colourways.

Fashionable
BUTTONS

MADE IN ENGLAND

Marine Waves Wrap

There are many exciting new fibres being used contemporarily in yarn; the merino wool used in this wrap has been combined with Seacell, a natural plant fibre derived from seaweed, which makes it perfect for this ocean-themed project. The Seacell contains minerals from seaweed, such as vitamin E and calcium, which are released when worn and can contribute to skin protection. This fits perfectly with the traditional idea that the fresh sea breeze is good for our health. The feather and fan stitch utilized at the ends of the wrap is beautifully organic, undulating in oceanlike waves of colour as the space-dyed yarn moves from one shade to the next. This striking use of technique and colour is a perfect example of how a static stitch structure can evoke rhythm and movement.

The wrap itself is extremely versatile; it can be worn in many different ways according to the occasion, practicality or mood. Knit a version with sleeves, or a straight wrap without shaping. Tie a dramatic knot in the front for an evening look, or wear casually loose and flowing for day wear, in different wraps around the body, or secured with a pin or brooch.

Note: Yarn quantities are based on average requirements and are therefore approximate. Yarn substitution: Any 4-ply yarn will do. Work a swatch!

Materials

- 7 x 112 g (4 oz) skeins Fleece Artist Sea Wool, 70% merino, 30% Seacell, 350 m (383 yd) in Nova Scotia
- Pair 3.25 mm (size 3) needles
- Set of four or five 3.25 mm (size 3) dpn or a 3.25-mm (size 3) 40-cm (16-in) long circular needle
- Stitch holders

Measurements

To fit bust

81–86	91–97	102–107	cm
32–34	36–38	40–42	in

Actual size all around

202	208	212	cm
79½	82	83½	in

Length to shoulder

45	47	49	cm
17¾	18½	19¼	in

Sleeve seam
12 cm (4¾ in)

Tension

28 sts and 37 rows to 10 cm (4 in) sq over st st on 3.25 mm (size 3) needles

33 sts and 44 rows to 10 cm (4 in) sq over feather and fan pattern on 3.25 mm (size 3) needles

Note
Figures in parentheses ( ) refer to larger sizes. Where only one set of figures is given, this applies to all sizes.

Right side

The right-hand side is worked in one piece from the right front edge to the mid back. Using 3.25 mm (size 3) needles and Fleece Artist Sea Wool, cast on 200 sts.

1st row: (RS) Knit.
2nd row: Purl.
3rd row: K1, * (k2tog) 3 times, (yo, k1) 6 times, (k2tog) 3 times, rep from * 10 times more, k1.
4th row: Knit.
Repeating 1st to 4th rows forms feather and fan pattern.

Cont in feather and fan pattern until right side measures 60 cm (23½ in), ending with a 4th row.
Next row: (RS) Knit.
Next row: (Decrease row WS) P5, (p2tog, p4, p2tog, p5) 15 times. 170 sts.

Beg with a knit row, cont in st st until right side measures 80 cm (31½ in), ending with a purl (WS) row. **

Place armhole

1st row: K42, cast off 50(53:56) sts (one stitch on RH needle after cast off), k77(74:71).
2nd row: P78(75:72). Cast on 50(53:56) sts, p42. 170 sts.
Cont in st st until right side measures 101(104:106) cm [39¾(41:41¾) in], ending with a knit (RS) row at the bottom edge.
Leave sts on a holder.

Left side

Work as for right side to **. 170 sts.

Place armhole

1st row: K78(75:72). Cast off 50(53:56) sts (one stitch on RH needle after cast off), k41.
2nd row: P42. Cast on 50(53:56) sts, k78(75:72). 170 sts.
Cont in st st until left side measures 101:104:106 cm [39¾(41:41¾) in] ending with a purl (WS) row at the bottom edge. Leave sts on a holder.

Join back and front

The join can be made without sleeves or after working the sleeves. Block each piece using the cold-water spray method. To do this, pin out your pieces to the required shape, spray and pat with your hands, then allow to dry naturally. Starting at the bottom edge, work Kitchener stitch, grafting both pieces together.

Sleeves (both alike)

Using a set of four or five 3.25 mm (size 3) dpn or a 3.25 mm (size 3) 40-cm (16-in)-long circular needle, and starting at underarm, pick up and knit 50(53:56) sts from each side of armhole. 100(106:112) sts.
PM at underarm for start of round and SM from LHN to RHN at the end of rounds.
Cont in st st (knit every rnd) until sleeve measures 12 cm (4¾ in), while at the same time dec 1 st on each side of underarm marker on 12th and 5 foll 4th rows as follows:
Sleeve decrease row: SM, k2, k2tog, knit to 4 sts before the marker, k2tog tbl, k2. Cast off purlwise (on RS). 88(94:100) sts. Weave in ends.

Westport Blocks

These building blocks are easy to make, and form a simple, effective educational toy for a young child. The inspiration comes from a row of weather-boarded beach houses in a seashore palette.

Square block

Using 5.5 mm (size 9) needles and any Yarn A, CO 14 sts and knit 26 rows garter st (2 rows of Yarn A, 2 rows of Yarn B).
Using A, k 1 row, p 1 row.
Cont in st st in this way, knit 15 rows total, ending with a k row.
Knit next row.
Work another 25 rows g st, alt bet 2 rows of A and 2 rows of B.
Next row: Using A, knit. Then p 1 row. Cont in st st in this way, knit 15 rows in total. Cast off all sts. Using A, CO 14 sts. Work 26 rows in garter st, cast off all sts. Make one more sq.

Triangular block

Using A, CO 14 sts and k 15 rows st st, beg and ending with a k row. K next row. Knit 15 rows st st, beg and ending with a k row. K next row. K 18 rows st st, beg with a k row. BO.

Using B, cast on 16 sts.
Work 2 rows st st, beg with a k row.
Next row: Change to B, k2tog, k to last 2 sts, k2tog. (14 sts). P next row. Maintaining st st, and changing colour every other row, decrease at each end of the following 5 k rows (4 sts). P 1 row.
Next row: Sl 1, k3tog, psso. Fasten off. Work one more triangle.

Assembly

Wrap the long strip around 4 sides of a foam cube and sew along one edge using mattress stitch.
Sew rem 2 sq over rem 2 sides of foam cube, using mattress stitch. Weave in the ends.

To make a triangle, cut one 7.5 cm (3 in) cube in half, diagonally. Take the long strip and wrap it around the three sq faces of the triangle made. Sew rem 2 triangle pieces to sides.

Materials

- Debbie Bliss Cashmerino Chunky, 55% merino wool, 33% microfibre, 12% cashmere, 50 g (1¾ oz) 65 m (71 yd). Yarn A: 1 ball each of 10 (sea green-blue), 11 (duck egg), 12 (lime), 14 (beige), 18 (navy), 21 (conch pink), 22 (powder pink), 23 (lavender), 24 (denim), 25 (sky blue), 26 (sand) and 28 (seaweed green)

Note: All shades can be used as yarn A; use one for each of 12 different blocks. Yarn B: 4 of 03 (beach hut white)

- 16 x 7.5 cm sq (3 in sq) blocks of foam (or alternatively use toy stuffing)
- Pair 5.5 mm (size 9) needles

Measurements

Each cube is roughly 7.5 cm (3 in) square

Tension

16 sts and 7 rows to 10 cm (4 in) square

Alternative yarns: We used a yarn that is machine-washable and with some man-made fibre in it to increase durability.

Caution: *Make sure the yarn you use is suitable for babies. Some yarns may leave excess fibre strands in a baby's mouth. Also make sure the foam/stuffing you use is non-toxic and flame-retardant.*

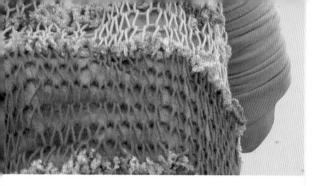

Materials

- **Yarn A: 2 x Debbie Bliss Cotton DK,**
  100% cotton, 50 g (1¾ oz), 80 m (87 yd)
  in 009, powder blue
  Yarn B: 1 x Colinette Isis, 100%
  viscose, 100 g (3½ oz), 100 m (109 yd)
  in seabreeze
  Yarn C: 1 x GGH Big Easy, 100%
  cotton, 50 g (1¾ oz), 70 m (77 yd) in
  011, grey

- Lining fabric to fit your finished bag

- 20 mm (size 35), 60-cm (24-in)
  circular needle

- 4 mm (size 6) needles

Measurements

Handle, approx 45 cm (17¾ in) long

Length of bag when hanging empty
approx 65 cm (25½ in) long

Tension

Approx 6 sts to 10 cm (4 in), over st st
without stretching

22 sts to 10 cm (4 in) over garter st on
handle using 4 mm (size 6) needles

*Yarn alternatives: The great thing about
this project is that practically any yarns will
do. The more holes you want, the finer the
yarn should be, or the larger the needles.
Fancy yarns added in stripes will lend great
detail and texture. Experiment!*

String Beach Bag

A handy hold-all to take to the beach, this bag can be folded up
and stored in a small space or pocket, then stretched out to hold a
remarkable number of things. Line with your choice of material, which
will show through the holes in the knitted fabric. The inspiration for this
technique comes from fishing nets and dried seaweed.

Bag

Using A and circ needles, CO 48sts
and join for working in the round. PM
at beg of rnd. Knit 4 rnds even.
Change to B held double and k 1 rnd.
Change to A and k 3 rnds.
Change to B held double and k 1 rnd.
Change to C and k 6 rows.
Change to B held double and k 1 row.
Change to C and work 3 rows.
Dec rnds: Cont in yarn C, dec 8 sts
as folls: (K4, k2tog) all around (40sts).
Next rnd: (K3, k2tog) all around (32sts).
Next rnd: (K2, k2tog) all around (24sts).
Next rnd: (K1, k2tog) all around (16sts).
Break off yarn; do not BO. Thread yarn
through rem 16 sts and pull tight to
close bottom of bag. Weave in all ends.

Handle

Using 4 mm (size 6) needles and yarn
A, pick up and knit 25 sts evenly
along approx 10 cm (4 in) of the cast-
on edge. Knit 1 row.
Next row: K2tog, k to last 2 sts, k2tog
(23 sts). K 2 rows.
Rep last 4 rows until 15 sts rem.
Work even in garter st until handle
measures approx 41 cm (16 in) long.
Inc 1 st at either end of next and
every 3rd row until there are 25 sts.
BO all sts. Attach end of handle
with mattress st to the exact
opposite edge of bag from the start
of the handle so that the bag is
symmetrical. Weave in all ends.

Finishing

Sew seam along two sides of a
rectangle of fabric for the lining.
Fold a 2.5 cm (1 in) hem under
the top edge and use a slip
stitch to attach the lining at the
inside top edge of the bag.

Frozen monochrome

Northern Europe is a harsh place to live from the winter solstice to the vernal equinox. North of the Arctic Circle the climate is extremely cold in winter, and the season lasts for up to six months. It is the land of the midnight sun, where in summer the sun never sets, yet in midwinter, in parts of Lapland, the sun never rises above the horizon, while the clear skies allow the breathtaking sight of the Aurora Borealis. This theme focuses on this bleak winter landscape and the knitting traditions born out of the cold climate.

The snow evokes a cool, clear colour palette of crisp whites, icy blues and sparkling silver. Collect as many different yarns in different shades of white as possible – it is surprising how many different versions there are. The resulting knitted items will be spectacular in their simplicity and subtlety and will allow any textures to stand out – a great idea for a warm winter blanket. Warm wools and fluffy yarns with their insulating properties create snug garments and accessories. The need for warm clothing is why the craft of knitting started in Scandinavia and other northern European countries related closely by climate and trade.

1 Cool blues evoke low light on icy landscapes. **2** The Norwegian eight-petalled rose design. **3** and **4** People who live and work in cold environments have developed traditions of making warm clothing.

Scandinavian design

One of the most popular knitted items from this region are Norwegian sweaters, worn by fashionable skiers throughout Europe and the United States. The multicolour techniques were developed by the ever practical Norwegians to enhance the insulating properties of the yarn.

The stranding of more than one colour of yarn creates a thick double fabric, while a twining technique uses two yarns alternated between every stitch, even if they are of the same colour, to make the fabric denser and warmer.

Tufting techniques were also developed to line the knitting, incorporating tufts of pure combed roving or unspun wool. The tuft is lightly twisted to roughly the same thickness as the yarn and can be used invisibly or as part of the pattern in a contrasting colour. The right side of the work is similar to a normal stocking stitch, but the reverse is fluffy. This texture was often exploited in hat designs, where the brim is turned back to contrast with the right side.

The multicolour technique is now widely known as Fair Isle, after the remote Scottish island positioned at the most northerly point of the UK, in the exposed North Sea, and close to Norway. This name is not always accurate, however, since

5 Undyed yarns come in various natural shades, from grey through brown to black. 6 Indigenous animals are well equipped for the conditions, and colours reflect their environment. 7 Lacy whites echo snow and ice patterns. 8 Fisherman's cables add insulation. 9 Black-and-white mittens are traditionally Scandinavian. 10 Cool blue horizons contain a surprising number of complementary hues. 11 Fluffy net stitches trap air, providing warmth. 12 Warm fleeces are ideally suited to cold climates.

8

9

10

11

12

many different cultures developed these knits simultaneously for the same reason – increased warmth. In fact, the resulting fabrics were very different in design.

Traditional Fair Isles of Scotland are very distinctive. Generally, very brightly dyed yarn was used – with patterns arranged in horizontal bands and colours and changing frequently – but with no more than two colours in each row. The most common colours were bright red, indigo blue, yellow, black and natural white.

In contrast, Norway's knits are mainly monochrome and are known for the all-over flecked 'lice' pattern, a great example of a simple yet striking design. The most famous of the Norwegian patterns is the floral motif of the eight-petaled rose, used in many ski sweaters. With the link to snow, many believe this to echo the shape of a snowflake. Figures, trees and reindeer are also commonly incorporated, often fairly small, and arranged symmetrically.

Original Aran sweaters from Ireland were highly decorated in intricate patterns reminiscent of Celtic knot work – the braids and twists are now known as cabling. This was not just for aesthetics; these patterns added to their insulating properties by trapping more air, and thus keeping the wearer warmer.

13 Feathered and chenille yarns echo the damp mosses of a spring thaw. **14** Heather-flecked greens and blues are a good way to replicate natural variegation. **15** The snow eventually melts to reveal fresh whites and an earthier palette of greys, browns and greens. **16** Frosted ice-crystal patterns recur in monochromatic Norwegian design.

Your Mood Board

Choose traditional braids in colours that reflect the landscape, along with natural yarns that echo the kinds available in these outlying regions. A burst of yellow lichen or blue sky can be copied with a button accent. Add snippets of yarn, swatches and inspiration from holiday photos or magazines.

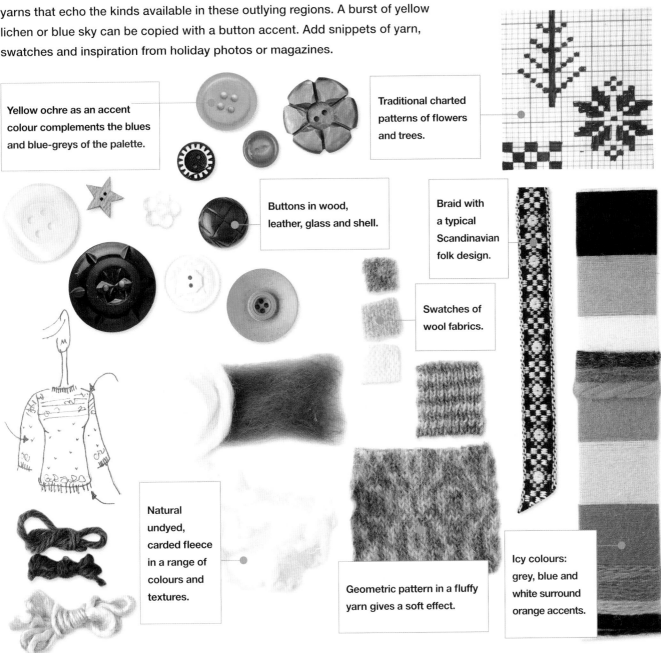

Yellow ochre as an accent colour complements the blues and blue-greys of the palette.

Traditional charted patterns of flowers and trees.

Buttons in wood, leather, glass and shell.

Braid with a typical Scandinavian folk design.

Swatches of wool fabrics.

Natural undyed, carded fleece in a range of colours and textures.

Geometric pattern in a fluffy yarn gives a soft effect.

Icy colours: grey, blue and white surround orange accents.

Scandinavian Mittens

Mittens have been knitted for many hundreds of years – their small size means they are a relatively quick and very portable project. Here, the pattern is a hybrid of many different cultures. The eight-petalled rose is generally thought of as Norwegian, but a very similar motif has been found in the Middle East, representing a more spiritual symbol: a star. The two-coloured corrugated rib is typical of Scandinavian knitting, and it is a stunning feature, especially since vertical stripes are rare in knitted pieces. The colours in the mittens have been chosen both with the images of snow and mountains in mind and the warmer, brighter colours used in the easternmost northern European countries, such as Finland.

The yarn is traditional Finnish mitten wool, which is available in an array of different colours. The yarn comes in huge skeins, which wind into large balls, and with the amount of colours used in these mittens, the yarn quantities would be enough to make a couple of pairs. That is just as well, because once you wear them, all your friends will be lusting after a pair!

Materials

- One each Vuorelman Satakieli 100% wool 4-ply, 100 g (3½ oz), 330 m (361 yd)
  Yarn A: 003 – cream
  Yarn B: 184 – gold
  Yarn C: 199 – pumpkin
  Yarn D: 499 – plum
  Yarn E: 631 – sky blue

- Set of four or five 2.75 mm (size 2) dpn

- Set of four or five 3.25 mm (size 3) dpn

- Stitch holders

Measurements

One size

Hand circumference 20 cm (8 in)

Length (from top of ribbing to tip)
21 cm (8¾ in)

Tension

35 sts and 32 rows = 10 cm (4 in) square over colour knitting worked in the round on 3.25 mm (size 3) needles or the size required to give the correct tension.

Note: Yarn quantities are based on average requirements and are therefore approximate. Yarn alternatives: any 4-ply or sock yarn.

Right mitten

Using a set of four or five 2.75 mm (size 2) dpn and Yarn B, cast on 64 sts. Distribute the sts over the needles in multiples of 2 or 4 and position the needles for working in the rnd. PM at beg of the rnd and slip the marker at the beg of every rnd.

1st rnd: [K2 using Yarn A, p2 using Yarn B] 16 times. Repeating 1st rnd forms 2 x 2 rib. Cont in 2 x 2 rib for 7 cm [2¾ in].

Next rnd: Using Yarn A, K18, k2tog, k18, [k5, k2tog] 3 times, k5. 60 sts. Break Yarn B. **

Change to 3.25 mm (size 3) needles.

Rnd 1: Knit 37 sts foll 1st row of chart for back of mitten working from right to left, then knit 23 sts foll 1st row of chart for palm of mitten working from right to left.

Rnds 2–14: Knit 37 sts foll chart for back of mitten working from right to left, then knit the sts foll chart for palm of mitten working from right to left and increasing for the thumb gore by working m1k where shown. 72 sts.

Rnds 15–49: Knit all 37 sts foll chart for back of mitten on page 54, working from right to left, then knit all 35 sts foll chart for front of mitten working from right to left.

Rnd 50: Ssk using Yarn C, knit next 33 sts foll chart for back of mitten, working from right to left, k2tog using Yarn C (35 sts rem for back of mitten), then ssk using Yarn A, knit next 31 sts foll chart for palm of mitten, working from right to left,

k2tog using Yarn A (33 sts rem for palm of mitten). 68 sts.

Rnds 51–66: Knit foll the chart for back of mitten, working from right to left, then knit foll chart for palm of mitten working from right to left while at the same time dec for top of mitten as established in the 50th rnd. 6 sts.

Rnd 67: Sl 1, k2 tog, psso using Yarn B, then sl 1, k2tog, psso using Yarn A. 2 sts. Break Yarn B and thread through rem st in Yarn B to fasten off, then break Yarn A and thread through rem st in Yarn A to fasten off. Weave in ends.

Right thumb

Carefully unravel the 17 sts worked in Yarn E at the top of the thumb gore on the palm of the mitten in the 17th rnd, transferring the 17 sts at the top of the thumb gore onto a st holder and the 17 sts on the palm onto another.

Rnd 1: With RS facing, using a set of four or five 3.25 mm (size 3) dpn and Yarn D, knit foll chart for the thumb on page 53 from right to left and starting with the thumb gore sts, pick up and knit 1 st between the palm and the thumb gore [st 1 on the chart for thumb], knit across all 17 thumb gore sts held on the first st holder foll chart from right to left [st 2 to st 18], using Yarn D pick up and knit 1 st between the thumb gore and the palm [st 19], then knit across all 17 palm sts held on the second st holder foll chart for the thumb, from right to left [st 20 to st 36]. 36 sts. PM for

beg of rnd.

Rnds 2–14: Knit all 36 sts foll the chart for thumb from right to left.

Rnd 15: Ssk using Yarn B, knit next 15 sts foll chart for thumb from right to left, k2tog using Yarn B, knit next 17 sts foll chart for thumb from right to left. 34 sts.

Rnd 16: Ssk using Yarn C, knit next 13 sts foll chart for thumb from right to left, k2tog using Yarn B, then ssk using Yarn A, knit next 13 sts foll chart for thumb from right to left, k2tog using Yarn A. 30 sts.

Rnds 17–22: Knit foll the chart for thumb working from right to left while at the same time dec for top of thumb as established in the 16th rnd. 6 sts.

Rnd 23: Sl 1, k2 tog, psso using Yarn E, then sl 1, k2tog, psso using Yarn A. 2 sts. Break Yarn C and thread through rem st in Yarn C to fasten off, then break Yarn A and thread through rem st in Yarn A to fasten off. Weave in ends.

Left mitten

Work as for right mitten to **. Change to 3.25 mm (size 3) needles.

Rnd 1: Knit all 37 sts foll 1st row of chart for back of mitten from left to right, then knit all 23 sts foll 1st row of chart for palm of mitten from left to right.

Rnds 7–67: Work as for right mitten but working both the chart for the back of the mitten and the chart for the palm of the mitten from left to right. Fasten off as for right mitten and weave in ends.

Left thumb

Carefully unravel the 17 sts worked in Yarn C at the top of the thumb gore on the palm of the mitten in rnd 17, transferring the 17 sts at the top of the thumb gore onto a st holder and the 17 sts on the palm onto another. Use the same chart as used for the right mitten to work the thumb.

Rnd 1: With RS facing, using a set of four or five 3.25 mm (size 3) dpn and yarn D, knit foll chart for the thumb from left to right and starting with the thumb palm sts, knit across all 17 palm sts held on the second st holder foll chart for the thumb from left to right [st 36 to st 20 on the chart for thumb], using Yarn D pick up and knit 1 st between the palm and thumb gore [st 19], knit across all 17 thumb gore sts held on the first st holder foll chart from left to right [st 18 to st 2], then using Yarn D pick up and knit 1 st between the thumb gore and the palm [st 1]. 36 sts. PM for beg of rnd.

Rnds 2–14: Knit all 36 sts foll the chart for thumb from left to right.

Rnd 15: K17 sts foll chart for thumb from left to right, ssk using Yarn B, knit next 15 sts foll chart for thumb from left to right, k2tog using Yarn B. 34 sts.

Rnd 16: Ssk using Yarn A, knit next 13 sts foll chart for thumb from left to right, k2tog using Yarn A, then ssk using Yarn B, knit next 13 sts foll chart for thumb, k2tog using Yarn B. 30 sts.

Thumb chart (same for both mittens)

Rnds 17–22: Knit foll the chart for thumb working from left to right while at the same time dec for top of thumb as established in the 16th rnd. 6 sts.

Rnd 23: Sl 1, k2tog, psso using Yarn A, then sl 1, k2tog, psso using Yarn E. 2 sts. Break Yarn A and thread through rem st in Yarn A to fasten off, then break Yarn E and thread through rem st in Yarn E to fasten off.

Finishing

Thread the tails from the fastening off onto wrong side of mitten so that the dec appears continuous. Weave in all loose ends.

Colour Key

☐ Yarn A – cream
▨ Yarn B – gold
▨ Yarn C – pumpkin
■ Yarn D – plum
▨ Yarn E – blue

Back of mitten

Two colours are used on every row, the background colour (Yarn A), and a second colour (Yarns B to E in sequence, as shown on the charts). Strand the yarn not in use on the WS (inside).

The mittens are worked in the round, using 4 or 5 needles. To obtain stocking st, knit every round.

Colour Key

- Yarn A – cream
- Yarn B – gold
- Yarn C – pumpkin
- Yarn D – plum
- Yarn E – blue
- Centre stitch

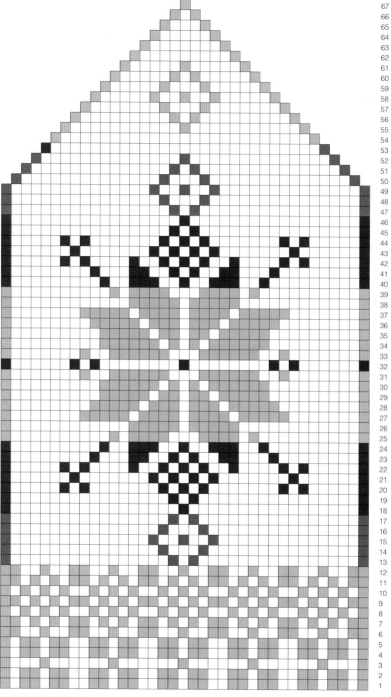

Front of right mitten (Reverse for left mitten)

This chart for the front (palm) of the mittens shows the thumb gore in an outlined box. On the first row of the chart, there are 5 sts for the thumb gore, increasing to 17 sts by the time row 4 of the chart has been worked. Use m1k, shown as M1 on the chart, to increase the sts. The band of 17 sts shown worked in Yarn E on the 17th row is for the position of the thumb, which will be worked later.

Colour Key

☐	Yarn A – cream
▨	Yarn B – gold
▨	Yarn C – pumpkin
■	Yarn D – plum
▨	Yarn E – blue
M1	Make one stitch knitwise (m1k)

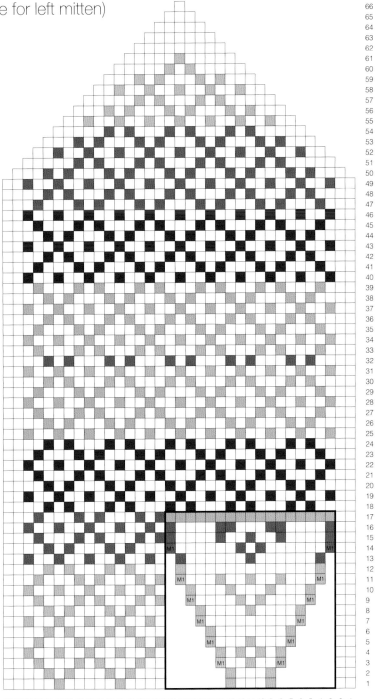

Materials

- 2 x Gedifra Sheela, 48% new wool, 48% acrylic, 4% nylon, 50 g (2 oz) 30 m (33 yd), in 4125 ecru
- 10 mm (size 15) 40-cm (16-in) long circular needle
- Wool lining fabric approx 22 x 35.5 cm (9 x 14 in)

Measurements

One size

Approx 22 cm (9 in) wide and 15 cm (6 in) diameter across openings for hands

Tension

Approx 7 sts and 9 rows to 10 cm (4 in)

Yarn alternatives: Any chunky-weight yarns. You can try knitting the muff in a smooth yarn instead of a bouclé, or a different type of fancy yarn, like an eyelash or chenille – experiment with the different textures.

Lammïn Muff

The image of ladies ice-skating on white winter days was the inspiration for this pattern, and it has been designed as a fun – and warm – alternative to gloves or mittens. The body heat generated from having both hands inside the muff means that it is often warmer than gloves. It is also practical because there is no searching for that elusive missing glove. This yarn is a dramatic bouclé, and when knitted up, it is reminiscent of snow, or the fur of a polar bear, and all with minimum effort – it uses the simplest garter stitch yet looks extremely dramatic, as though you have slaved over the knitting.

To make

Cast on 35 sts using 10 mm (size 15) needles and join for working in the round, placing a marker at the end of the round and knit for 22 cm (9 in) even. Cast off all sts and weave in ends.

Finishing

Line the muff with the wool fabric, as follows: Cut a piece of fabric approx to fit the inside of the muff, allowing 2 cm (¾ in) for hem. This should be about 22 cm (8½ in) wide and 35.5 cm (14 in) long. Turn back hem on both long sides and secure. Join the rectangle into a tube by sewing together the two short edges. Place inside the muff, with right side showing. Attach around each opening using secure backstitches.

Materials

- **Garnstudio Karisma, 100% pure new wool, 50 g (2 oz), 110 m (120 yd)**
  Yarn A: 8 x shade 1 (off white)
  Yarn B: 2 x shade 37 (dark grey blue)
  Yarn C: 2 x shade 30 (light blue)
  Yarn D: 2 x shade 56 (dark brown)

- **3 mm (size 3) and 3.5 mm (size 4) circular knitting needles 60-cm (24-in) long**

- **Set of four or five 3 mm (size 3) and 3.5 mm (size 4) dpn**

- **Stitch holders**

- **Sewing thread to match Yarn A**

Measurements

81–86	91–97	102–107	cm
32–34	36–38	40–42	in

Actual size

92	103	114	cm
36¼	40½	44¾	in

Length to shoulder

60	62	64	cm
23½	24½	25	in

Sleeve seam
43 cm (17 in)

Tension

22 sts and 30 rnds to 10 cm (4 in) sq over st st and lice st on 3.5 mm (size 4) needles. 24 sts and 28 rnds to 10 cm (4 in) sq over all other colour charts on 3.5 mm (size 4) needles

Astrid Sweater

This wonderful pattern is an updated version of the classic ski sweater. The adorable tree motif and traditional lice pattern are utilized to stunning effect with more abstract motifs, making the decoration interesting without the danger of becoming a clichéd novelty holiday sweater.

A relatively neutral colour palette adheres to the typical muted tones of Norwegian design, yet the traditional creams and browns have been added to icy blues inspired by the theme of ice and snow.

The pattern has been knitted in a traditional Scandinavian way: with steeks. This means that the whole body of the sweater can be knitted in one tube and then cut to make the holes for the neck and sleeves. This method of knitting is extremely economical, resulting in little wasted time and effort.

The fibre used is also Norwegian – a beautiful vintage wool that has been a staple for many, many years in traditional Norwegian sweaters.

Yarn alternatives: Good yarn substitutions are pure wool or mostly wool fibres, which are less likely to fray when cut when it comes to the steeks. The weight will be any DK or sportweight yarn.

Figures in parentheses ( ) refer to larger sizes. When only one set of figures is given, it applies to all sizes.

The sweater is worked as one piece in the round using a circular needle or, if preferred, a set of 4 or 5 dpn. To obtain stocking st, knit every row.

The armholes are worked as steeks, and the sleeves are sewn in afterward. The neck opening is also worked as a steek.

The colour motifs use two colours on every round: the background colour (Yarn A) and a second colour (Yarns B, C or D, as directed or as shown on the charts). The third colour used in chart 1 can be embroidered afterwards. Strand the yarn not in use on the WS (inside) of the sweater.

Lice st

Rnds 1–2: Knit using Yarn A.
Rnd 3: * K5 using Yarn A, k1 using Yarn B; rep from * to end.
Rnds 4–5: Knit using Yarn A.
Rnd 6: * K2 using Yarn A, k1 using Yarn B, k3 using Yarn A; rep from * to end.
Repeating 1st to 6th rounds forms lice stitch.

Body

Using a 3 mm (size 3) circular needle and Yarn B, cast on 208(232:256) sts. PM at the beginning and halfway through the rnd and slip marker at every rnd.
Rnds 1–2: * K2, p2; rep from * to end. Break Yarn B.
Join Yarn A.
Rnds 3–15: * K2, p2; rep from * to end. Drop Yarn A. Join Yarn D.
Rnds 16–17: * K2, p2; rep from *

to end. Break Yarn D. Rib should measure 5 cm (2½ in).
Change to a 3.5 mm (size 4) circular needle and Yarn A.
Rnd 1: (Inc rnd) [K3, m1k, k7, m1k, k3] 16(0:0) times, [(k5, m1k, k4) twice, (k4, m1k, k4) 10 times, (k4, m1k, k5) twice] 0(2:0) times, [(k6, m1k, k5) twice, k5, m1k, k5] 0(0:8) times. 240(260:280) sts.
Rnd 2: Work all 10 sts from first row of Chart 1, 24(26:28) times, reading the chart from right to left.
Rnds 3–12: Work all 10 sts from 2nd to 11th rows of Chart 1, 24(26:28) times, reading the chart from right to left on every rnd.
Rnd 13: (dec rnd) [Using Yarn A [k5, k2tog] 1(0:0) time, [k7, k2tog] 12(0:0) times, [k9, k2tog] 0(11:1) times, [k13, k2tog] 0(0:8) times, k5(9:9)] twice. 214(238:262) sts.
Beginning with the 1st rnd, work 0(3:6) rnds in lice st, setting the position of the pattern as follows: [Work all 6 sts from Chart 2 17(19:21) times then work 1st to 5th sts from Chart 2 once, reading the chart from right to left on every round] twice. 214(238:262) sts.

Shape waist

Maintain continuity of lice st throughout waist shaping.
Rnd 1: [1st(4th:1st) row of lice stitch from Chart 2] [K1 k2tog, k101(113:125), ssk, k1] twice. 210(234:258) sts.
Rnd 2: Using Yarn A, knit.
Rnd 3: Patt, beginning the round [K4(1:4) using Yarn A, k1 using Yarn

B, [k5 using Yarn A, k1 using Yarn B] 16(19:20) times, k4(1:4) using Yarn A] twice. Maintain the lice st pattern.
Rnd 4: Using Yarn A, [K1, k2tog, k99(111:123), ssk, k1] twice. 206(230:254) sts.
Rnds 5–6: Patt.
Cont in lice stitch patt and dec as est on next rnd and on 6 foll 3rd rnds. 178(202:226) sts. Work 9 rounds patt without shaping.
Next rnd: [K1, m1k, k87(99:111), m1k, k1] twice. 182(206:230) sts.
Cont in lice stitch patt and inc as est on 5 foll 4th rnds. 202(226:250) sts.

Cont in lice st until body measures 40(40:42 cm) [15¾(15¾, 16½) in] ending with a 6th row of lice st. The Yarn B stitches from the 6th row of lice stitch at 40(42:44 cm) [15¾(16½:17⅓) in] will form the bottom stitch of a triangle, which will be completed in the 3 foll rnds.

Size 32–34 in [81–86 cm]

Next rnd: * Next rnd: [[K1 using Yarn B, k3 using Yarn A, k2 using Yarn B] 16 times, k1 using Yarn B, k3 using Yarn A, k1 using Yarn B] twice.
Next rnd: [[K2 using Yarn B, k1 using Yarn A, k3 using Yarn B] 16 times, k2 using Yarn B, k1 using Yarn A, k2 using Yarn B] twice.
Next rnd: Using Yarn B, knit.
Next rnd: Using Yarn C, knit.
Next rnd: Using Yarn A, knit.
Next rnd: (increase round) Using Yarn C, [k8, m1, (k12, m1) 7 times, k9)] twice. 218 sts.
Body should measure 42 cm (16½ in).

Form steeks for armholes

Rnd 1: Using Yarn A, cast on 10 sts to LHN at beginning of round. PM to mark new beginning of round.

Join Yarn C and work [k1 using Yarn A, k1 using Yarn C] 5 times across the 10 sts. SM which marked the original beginning of round now marks end of first steek. Work first 12 sts from first row of Chart 3, 9 times then 13th stitch from first row of Chart 3 once, reading the chart from right to left. SM which marked the original halfway through the round now marks beginning of second steek. Using Yarn A, cast on 10 sts to LHN. [K1 using Yarn A, k1 using Yarn C] 5 times across the 10 sts. PM on RHN to mark the end of the second steek. Work first 12 sts from first row of Chart 3, 9 times then 13th stitch from first row of Chart 3 once. 238 sts.

For all following rounds, when working with two colours work the 10 sts of all the steeks in alternate colours (like a chequerboard) and when changing a yarn colour, change on the 6th stitch of the first steek. Slip all markers where they occur in the round.

Rnd 2: [[K1 using Yarn C, k1 using Yarn A] 5 times across the steek, work first 12 sts from 2nd row of Chart 3, 9 times then 13th stitch from second row of Chart 3 once] twice.

Rnds 3–13: Cont working steeks and rows 3 to 13 from Chart 3 in patt as established, reading every row from

Chart 3 from right to left. Chart 3 completed.

Rnd 14: Using Yarn B, knit.
Rnd 15: Using Yarn D, knit.
Rnd 16: Using Yarn B, knit.
Rnd 17: [Work 10 steek sts, work first 12 sts from first row of Chart 4, 9 times then 13th stitch from first row of Chart 4 once] twice.
Rnd 18: [Work 10 steek sts, work first 12 sts from 2nd row of Chart 4, 9 times then 13th stitch from first row

of Chart 4 once] twice.
Rnds 19–28: Cont working steeks and rows 3 to 12 from Chart 4 in patt as established, reading every row from Chart 4 from right to left. Chart 4 completed.

Sizes 91–97, 102–107 cm [36–38 and 40–42 in]
Form steeks for armholes
Rnd 1: Using Yarn A, cast on 10 sts to LHN at beginning of round. PM to mark new beginning of round. Work [k1 using Yarn A, k1 using Yarn B] 5 times across the 10 sts. SM which marked the original beginning of round and which now marks end of first steek. [K1 using Yarn B, k3 using Yarn A, k2 using Yarn B] (18:20) times, k1 using Yarn B, k3 using Yarn A, k1 using Yarn B. SM which marked the original halfway through the round and which now marks beginning of second steek. Using Yarn A, cast on 10 sts to LHN. [K1 using Yarn A, k1 using Yarn B] 5 times across the 10 sts. PM on RHN to mark the end of the second steek. [K1 using Yarn B, k3 using Yarn A, k2 using Yarn B] (18:20) times, k1 using Yarn B, k3 using Yarn A, k1 using Yarn B.

For all following rounds, when working with two colours work the 10 sts of the steeks in alternate colours (like a chequerboard) and when changing a yarn colour, change on the 6th stitch of the first steek. Slip all markers where they occur in the round.

Rnd 2: [[K1 using Yarn B, k1 using Yarn A] 5 times across the steek, [K2 using Yarn B, k1 using Yarn A, k3 using Yarn B] (18:20) times, k2 using Yarn B, k1 using Yarn A, k2 using Yarn B] twice.
Rnd 3: Using Yarn B, knit.
Rnd 4: Using Yarn C, knit.
Rnd 5: Using Yarn A, knit.
Rnd 6: (increase round) Using Yarn C, [k10 steek sts, k(7:10), m1, [k14, m1] (7:0) times, [k15, m1] (0:7) times, k(8:10)] twice. (262:286) sts.
Rnd 7: Work the 10 steek sts joining Yarn A, work first 12 sts from first row of Chart 3 (10:11) times then 13th stitch from first row of Chart 3 once, work 10 steek sts, work first 12 sts from first row of Chart 3 (10:11) times then 13th stitch from first row of Chart 3 once.
Rnd 8: [Work 10 steek sts, work first 12 sts from 2nd row of Chart 3 (10:11) times then 13th stitch from second row of Chart 3 once] twice.
Rnds 9–19: Cont working steeks and rows 3 to 13 from Chart 3 in patt as established, reading every row from Chart 3 from left to right. Chart 3 completed.

Rnd 20: Using Yarn B, knit.
Rnd 21: Using Yarn D, knit.
Rnd 22: Using Yarn B, knit.
Rnd 23: [Work 10 steek sts, work first 12 sts from first row of Chart 4 (10:11) times then 13th stitch from first row of Chart 4 once] twice.
Rnd 24: [Work 10 steek sts, work first 12 sts from 2nd row of Chart 4 (10:11) times then 13th stitch from first row

of Chart 4 once] twice.

Rnds 25–34: Cont working steeks and rows 3 to 12 from Chart 4 in patt as established, reading every row from Chart 4 from left to right. Chart 4 completed.

Shape neck (all sizes)

Rnd 1: Using Yarn B, knit 10 steek sts, k45(50:55) sts for left front neck, slip centre 19(21:23) sts onto a holder for front neck, PM on RHN to mark beg of neck steek, cast on 10 sts to LHN, knit these 10 sts for neck steek, PM to mark end of neck steek, knit to end. The 19(21:23) sts at centre front neck have the last 3(10:5) sts of a patt rep, 12(0:12) sts of a whole patt rep, and the first 4(11:6) sts of a patt rep worked on the previous round. 229(251:273) sts.

Rnd 2: Using Yarn D, knit to 2 sts before the neck steek, ssk, knit 10 neck steek sts, k2tog, knit to end. 227(249:271) sts.

Rnd 3: Using Yarn B, knit to 2 sts before the neck steek, ssk, knit 10 neck steek sts, k2tog, knit to end. 225(247:269) sts.

Rnd 4: Working all steek sts in alternate colours as before, work 10 steek sts, reading the first row from Chart 5 from right to left, work 1st to 12th sts 3(3:4) times, then work 1st to 5th(1st to 10th:1st to 3rd) sts once, ssk, work 10 steek sts, k2tog, work 9th to 12th(4th to 12th:11th and 12th) sts from first

row of Chart 5 once, work 1st to 12th sts 3(3:4) times, work 13th st once, work 10 steek sts, work the 1st to 12th sts from first row of Chart 5 9(10:11) times, work the 13th st once. 223(245:267) sts.
4th round sets the pattern.

Rnds 5–14: Cont working in patt, working rows 2 to 11 of Chart 5, dec 1 st at neck edge as established of the 5th, 7th, 9th, 11th and 13th(5th to 9th, 11th and 13th:5th to 13th) rounds of neck shaping [the 2nd, 4th, 6th, 8th and 10th(2nd to 6th, 8th and 10th:2nd to 10th) rows of Chart 5]. 213(231:249) sts.
Chart 5 completed.
Break Yarn D.

Rnd 15: Using Yarn A, knit to 2 sts before neck steek, ssk, knit 10 steek sts, k2tog, knit to end. 211(229:247) sts.

Rnd 16: (dec round) Using Yarn A, knit 10 steek sts, K0(0:1) [k3, k2tog, k4] 4(1:0) times, [k4, k2tog, k4] 0(3:4) times, k0(0:1), knit 10 steek sts, K0(0:1), [k4, k2tog, k4] 0(3:4) times, [k4, k2tog, k3] 4(1:0) times, k0(0:1), knit 10 steek sts, [k4, k2tog, k3] 12(0:0) times, [k4, k2tog, k4] 0(12:0) times, [k5, k2tog, k4] 0(0:12) times, k1. 191(209:227) sts.

Rnd 17: Work 10 steek sts, k3 using Yarn A, [k1 using Yarn B, k5 using Yarn A] 4(5:5) times, k1(0:1) using Yarn B, k2(0:2) using Yarn A, ssk using Yarn A(Yarn B:Yarn A), work 10 steek sts, k2tog using Yarn A(Yarn B:Yarn A), k2(0:2) using Yarn A, k1(0:1) using Yarn B, [k5 using Yarn A, k1 using Yarn B] 4(5:5) times, k3 using Yarn A, work 10 steek sts, k3 using Yarn A, [k1 using Yarn B, k5 using Yarn A] 15(17:19) times, k1 using Yarn B, k3 using Yarn A. 189(207:225) sts.

Rnd 18: Work 10 steek sts, k2 using Yarn A, [k3 using Yarn B, k3 using Yarn A] 4(5:5) times, k3(2:3) using Yarn B, K2(0:2) using Yarn A, work 10 steek sts, k2(0:2) using Yarn A, k3(2:3) using Yarn B, [k3 using Yarn A, k3 using Yarn B] 4(5:5) times, k2 using Yarn A, work 10 steek sts, k2 using Yarn A, [k3 using Yarn B, k3 using Yarn A] 15(17:19) times, k3 using Yarn B, k2 using Yarn A.

Rnd 19: Work 10 steek sts, k1 using Yarn A, [k5 using Yarn B, k1 using Yarn A] 4(5:5) times, k4(1:4) using Yarn B, ssk using Yarn B, work 10 steek sts, k2tog using Yarn B, k4(1:4) using Yarn B, [k1 using Yarn A, k5 using Yarn B] 4(5:5) times, k1 using Yarn A, work 10 steek sts, [k1 using Yarn A, k5 using Yarn B] 16(18:20) times, k1 using Yarn A. 187(205:223) sts.

Rnd 20: Using Yarn B, knit.
Rnd 21: Using Yarn C, knit.
Rnd 22: Using Yarn C, sl 1 steek stitch, cast off 8 steek sts [1 st on RHN – the 10th steek stitch], k30(33:36) [right front neck], k1 steek stitch, cast off 8 steek sts [one st on RHN – the 10th steek stitch],

k30(33:36) [left front neck],
k1 steek stitch, cast off 8 steek
sts [one st on RHN – the 10th
steek stitch], k97(109:121) [back],
knit the steek stitch slipped at
beg of round. Armhole should
measure 19(20:20 cm) [7½(8:8
in)] body should measure
60(62:64 cm) [23½ (24½:25) in].

Join shoulders

Turn the sweater inside out. Slip
32(35:38) sts [1 armhole steek stitch
and 31(34:37) body sts] from back
right shoulder onto a 3.5 mm (size
4) dpn and slip 32(35:38) sts [one
armhole steek stitch, 30(33:36)
body sts, 1 neck steek stitch]
from right front shoulder onto a
second 3.5 mm (size 4) dpn. Cast
off both sets of stitches together
using the three-needle cast off
method, working from shoulder
to neck edge. Slip the 35(41:47) sts
for centre back neck onto a stitch
holder. Cast off 32(34:37) sts for
back right shoulder and 32(34:37)
sts for front right shoulder using the
three-needle cast off method, again
working from shoulder to neck.

Make armholes (both alike)

Turn the sweater right side out.
Using a length of Yarn D, make a
tacking line down the centre of the
steek (between the 5th and 6th sts).
Using sewing thread matching Yarn
A, work a line of back sts between
the first st and 2nd st of the steek
and another between the 9th and
10th sts of the steek. If preferred, the

sewing can be done using a sewing
machine. Make sure that all sts are
secure. If desired, work a second or
third line of sts over the first line.
Cut the steek along the tacking line
between cast-on and cast-off edge.

Sleeves (both alike)

Using a set of 3 mm (size 3) dpn and
Yarn B, cast on 52(60:60) sts. PM at
beginning of rnd.
Rnd 1–2: *K2, p2; rep from * to end.
Break Yarn B. Join Yarn A.
Rnds 3–15: *K2, p2; rep from * to end.
Drop Yarn A. Join Yarn D.
Rnds 16–17: *K2, p2; rep from * to
end. Rib should measure 5 cm (2½ in).
Change to 3.5 mm (size 4) needles.
Rnd 1: (inc round) Using Yarn A, [k5,
m1k] 1(0:0) times, [k6, m1k] 7(0:0)
times, [k5, m1k, k6, m1k] 0(5:5) times,
k5. 60(70:70) sts.
Rnd 2: Work 10 sts from 1st row of
Chart 1, 6(7:7) times, reading chart
from right to left.
Rnd 3–12: Work 10 sts from 2nd to
11th rows of Chart 1, 6(7:7) times.
Rnd 13: (dec round) Using Yarn A [k5,
k2tog] 1(0:0) times, [k4, k2tog] 8(1:1)
times, [k8, k2tog] 0(6:6) times, k5(4:4).
51(63:63) sts.
Rnd 14: Using Yarn A work all 6 sts
from 2nd row of Chart 2 8(10:10)
times then 1st to 3rd sts from 2nd
row of Chart 2 once. 14th round sets
the position of lice stitch.
Cont working in lice stitch from
Chart 2 for a further 64 rounds while
at the same time inc 1 st at beg
[as k1, m1k] and end [as m1k, k1]

of the next rnd and 8 foll 7th rnds,
taking inc sts into the lice stitch patt,
ending on a 6th row of lice stitch.
69(81:81) sts. Sleeve should measure
approx 31 cm (12 in).

The Yarn B stitches from the 6th
row of lice stitch just worked will
form the bottom stitch of a triangle
[as was worked on the body of the
sweater], which will be completed in
the 3 foll rnds.
Rnd 79: [K1 using Yarn B, k3 using
Yarn A, k2 using Yarn B], 11(13:13)
times, k1 using Yarn B, k2 using A.
Rnd 80: [K2 using Yarn B, k1 using
Yarn A, k3 using Yarn B] 11(13:13)
times, k2 using Yarn B, k1 using A.
Rnd 81: Using Yarn B, knit.
Rnd 82: Using Yarn A, knit.
Rnd 83: (inc rnd) Using Yarn C,
k7(5:5), m1k, [k8, m1k] 7(0:0) times,
[k10, m1k] 0(7:7) times, k6(6:6).
77(89:89) sts.
Rnd 84: Work 5th to 12th sts from
first row of Chart 3, work all 12 sts
from first row of Chart 3, 5(6:6) times,
work 1st to 9th sts from first row of
Chart 3, reading from left to right.
Rnd 85–96: Cont in patt as set,
working 2nd to 13th rows of Chart
3 reading chart from right to left on
every round while at the same time
inc 1 st at both ends of round on the
85th, 88th, 92nd and 95th rnds [2nd,
5th, 9th and 12th rows of Chart 3].
85(97:97) sts.
Rnd 97: Using Yarn B, knit.
Rnd 98: Using Yarn D, knit.
Rnd 99: Using Yarn B, knit.
Rnd 100–111: Starting with the first

Astrid charts 1–5

Charts 2 to 5 appear from the bottom up, as they are seen on the sweater.

Colour Key

☐ Yarn A—off white

■ Yarn B—dark gray blue

☐ Yarn C—light blue

▨ Yarn D—dark brown

Chart 1

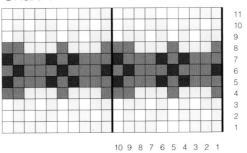

Repeat these 10 sts

Chart 5

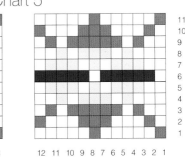

Chart 4

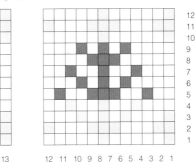

Chart 3

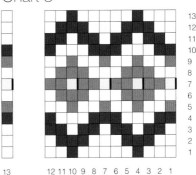

Repeat these 12 sts

Chart 2: Lice stitch and triangle

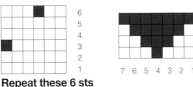

Repeat these 6 sts

row, work 1st to 12th sts of Chart 4 7(8:8) times then 13th st of Chart 4 once.
Rnd 112–113: Using Yarn A, knit.

Hem at top of sleeve

Turn work inside out so that the WS of sleeve is outermost and work the top of sleeve hem.
Rnd 114–119: Using Yarn A, knit. Cast off loosely.

Neckband

Turn the sweater right side out and prepare the front neck steeks as for the armhole steeks.

When picking up sts for the neckband, insert the needle between the edge st of the main fabric and the steek st adjacent to it.

Using a set of 4 or 5 3 mm (size 3) dpn and Yarn D, pick up and knit 22 sts down left front neck, knit across 19 sts from holder at centre front neck, pick up and knit 22 sts up right front neck, 1 st from back neck, knit across 35 sts centre back neck, pick up and

knit 1 st from back neck. 100 sts.
Rnds 1–2: Using Yarn D, * k2, p2; rep from * to end.
Rnds 3–6: Using Yarn A, * k2, p2; rep from * to end.
Rnds 7–8: Using Yarn B, * k2, p2; rep from * to end.
Using Yarn B, cast off in rib. Weave in ends.

Finishing

Turn the sweater inside out.
Trim steeks to 2 or 3 stitches wide.
Do not cut the previous stitching.
Fold neck steek to the WS and sew into position by oversewing or using herringbone/cross-stitch or blanket stitch. If preferred, trim steeks as you go. Set in sleeves using mattress stitch, or backstitch, along the round before the start of the hem at the top of the sleeve.

Fold the hem over the arm steek and sew into place with a whip stitch. Pin sweater to size, cover with a damp cloth and leave until dry.

Cropped Aran Jacket

The Aran Isles of Ireland are a cold, desolate place, and in past times hand spinning and knitting wool from the indigenous sheep meant the resulting yarn had the same insulating qualities. This pattern uses a British yarn from a rare breed of sheep. The Teeswater is a magnificent-looking animal with a long, lustrous fleece, and this yarn is lovingly handspun by one woman – Debbie Fisher of Hawthorne Heritage Crafts – as it originally would have been in the Aran Isles.

The original Aran sweaters were highly decorated in intricate patterns reminiscent of Celtic knot work – the braids and twists now known as cabling. Certain Aran designs were distinctive to different families because the stitches were not written down but instead passed down through the generations. This design uses a variety of different cables in a modern and feminine bolero style.

Yarn alternatives: Any Aran or worsted-weight yarn. You do not have to stick to pure wool fibres, but try to use a fairly smooth-spun yarn, since fancy yarns may not allow the cable patterning to show up clearly. The same goes for dark-coloured yarns.

Materials

- 6 (7, 8) x 100 g (3½ oz) balls approx 155 m (170 yd) Hawthorne Heritage Crafts 100% Teeswater wool undyed and handspun
- 5 mm (size 8) needles or 5 mm (size 8) circular needle 60 cm (24 in) long
- Cable needle
- Stitch holders
- Undyed fleece or yarn to make button

Measurements

To fit bust

81–86	91–97	102–107	cm
32–34	36–38	40–42	in

Actual size

98	108	118	cm
38½	42½	46½	in

Length to shoulder

41	42	43	cm
16	16½	17	in

Sleeve seam 30 cm (12 in)

Tension

18½ sts and 24½ rows to 10 cm (4 in) sq over st st on 5 mm (size 8) needles or the size required to give the tension

24 sts and 26 rows to 10 cm (4 in) sq over cabled rib pattern on 5 mm (size 8) needles or the size required for tension

Tension for st st and cabled rib will give correct tension for the cable patterns.

Notes

Figures in parentheses ( ) refer to larger sizes. When only one set of figures is given, it applies to all sizes.

The jacket/shrug is made in one piece to the armholes. The front and back widths, after casting off for the square armholes, are the same for all sizes. The sleeve top lengths are longer for each size to fit.

Special abbreviations

C2L/C2R – cable 2 sts left/right. Slip next st onto a cn and hold at front/back of work, k1 from LH needle, k1 from cn. **C3L** – cable 3 sts left. Slip next st onto a cn and hold at front of work, k2 from LH needle, k1 from cn. **C3R** – cable 3 sts right. Slip next 2 sts onto a cn and hold at back of work, k1 from needle, k2 from cn. **C4B** – cable 4 sts back. Slip next 2 sts onto a cable and hold at back of work, k2 from LH needle, k2 from cn. **C4F** – cable 4 sts front. Slip next 2 sts onto a cable and hold at front of work, k2 from LH needle, k2 from cn. **C6B** – cable 6 sts back. Slip next 3 sts onto a cable and hold at back of work, k3 from LH needle, k3 from cn. **C6F** – cable 6 sts front. Slip next 3 sts onto a cable and hold at front of work, k3 from LH needle, k3 from cn.

m1k – make one stitch by picking up the bar between the needles and knitting into the back of it.

MB – make bobble by working into the front, back and then front again of the next stitch, [turn and knit these 3 sts] 3 times, turn and then sl 1, k2tog, psso to complete the bobble.

T2L/T2R – twist 2 sts left/right. Slip next stitch onto a cn and hold at front/back of work, p1/k1 from left hand needle, k1/p1 from cn. **T3B** – twist 3 sts back. Slip next stitch onto a cn and hold at back of work, k2 from left hand needle, p1 from cn. **T3F** – twist 3 sts front. Slip next 2 stitches onto a cn and hold at front of work, p1 from left hand needle, k2 from cn.

T4B – twist 4 sts back. Slip next 2 stitches onto a cn and hold at back of work, k2 from left hand needle, p2 from cn. **T4F** – twist 4 sts front. Slip next 2 stitches onto a cn and hold at front of work, p2 from left hand needle, k2 from cn. **T5B** – twist 5 sts back. Slip next 3 stitches onto a cn and hold at back of work, k2 from left hand needle, p3 from cn. **T5F** – twist 5 sts front. Slip next 2 stitches onto a cn and hold at front of work, p3 from left hand needle, k2 from cn.

Stitch patterns

Panel 1 (Cabled rib pattern)

Worked over 4 sts and 2 rows.

Row 1: (RS) * C2R, C2L.
Row 2: P4.

Repeating 1st and 2nd rows forms the pattern.

Panel 2 (Winding cable)

Worked over 12 sts and 25 rows.

Row 1: (RS) P2, k4, p2, k2, p2.
Row 2: (WS) K2, p2, k2, p4, k2.
Row 3: P2, C4F, p2, T4F.
Rows 4–6: P2, k4, p4, k2.
Row 7: P2, C4F, p4, k2.
Rows 8–10: P2, k4, p4, k2.
Row 11: P2, C4F, p2, T4B.
Row 12: K2, p2, k2, p4, k2.
Row 13: P2, k2, T4F, k2, p2.
Row 14: K2, p4, k2, p2, k2.
Row 15: T4B, p2, C4B, p2.
Rows 16–18: K2, p4, k4, p2.
Row 19: K2, p4, C4B, p2.
Rows 20–22: K2, p4, k4, p2.
Row 23: T4F, p2, C4B, p2.
Row 24: K2, p4, k2, p2, k2.
Row 25: P2, k2, T4B, k2, p2.

Rows 2 to 25 form the pattern.

Panel 3 (OXO cable)

Worked over 8 sts and 16 rows.

Row 1: (RS) K2, m1k, k2, m1k, k2. 8 sts.
Row 2: P8.
Row 3: C4F, C4B.
Row 4: P8.
Row 5: K8.
Row 6: P8.
Row 7: C4F, C4B.
Row 8: P8.
Row 9: K8.
Row 10: P8.

Row 11: C4B, C4F.
Rows 12–15: Repeat 8th to 11th rows.
Rows 16–18: Repeat 4th to 6th rows.
Rows 3 to 18 form the pattern.

Panel 4 (Rope cable right)
Worked over 6 sts and 6 rows.
Row 1: (RS) K6.
Row 2: P6.
Row 3: K6.
Row 4: P6.
Row 5: C6B.
Row 6: P6.
Rows 1 to 6 form the pattern.

Panel 5A (Braid cable right)
Worked over 9 sts and 4 rows.
Row 1: (RS) Slip 2 sts onto a CN and leave at back of work, [k1, m1k, k1] from LHN, [k1, m1k, k1] from CN, [k1, m1k, k1] from LHN. 9 sts.
Row 2: P9.
Row 3: K3, C6F.
Row 4: P9.
Row 5: C6B, K3.
Row 6: P9.
Rows 3 to 6 form the pattern.

Panel 5B (Braid cable left)
Worked over 9 sts and 4 rows.
Row 1: (RS) [K1, m1, k1] from LHN, slip 2 sts onto a CN and leave at front of work, [k1, m1k, k1] from LHN, [k1, m1k, k1] from CN.
Row 2: P9.
Row 3: C6B, k3.
Row 4: P9.
Row 5: K3, C6F.
Row 6: P9.
Rows 3 to 6 form the pattern.

Panel 6 (Rope cable left)
Worked over 6 sts and 6 rows.
Row 1: (RS) K6.
Row 2: P6.
Row 3: K6.
Row 4: P6.
Row 5: C6F.
Row 6: P6.
Rows 1 to 6 form the pattern.

Panel 7 (Honeycomb cable)
Worked over 8 sts and 8 rows.
Row 1: (RS) K2, m1k, k2, m1k, k2. 8 sts.
Row 2: P8.
Row 3: C4B, C4F.
Row 4: P8.
Row 5: K8.
Row 6: P8.
Row 7: C4F, C4B.
Row 8: P8.
Row 9: K8.
Row 10: P8.
Rows 3 to 10 form the pattern.

Panel 8 (Claw)
Worked over 6 sts and 4 rows.
Row 1: (RS) K6.
Row 2: P6.
Row 3: C3R, C3L.
Row 4: P6.
Rows 1 to 4 form the pattern.

Panel 9 (Waves and bobbles)
Worked over 26 sts and 12 rows.
Row 1: (RS) P2, T3B, p5, C6B, p5, T3F, p2.
Row 2: K2, p2, k6, p6, k6, p2, k2.
Row 3: P1, T3B, p4, T5B, T5F, p4, T3F, p1.
Row 4: K1, p2, k5, p3, k4, p3, k5, p2, k1.
Row 5: T3B, p3, T5B, p4, T5F, p3, T3F.
Row 6: P2, k1, MB, k2, p3, k8, p3, k2, MB, k1, p2.

Row 7: T3F, p3, k3, p8, k3, p3, T3B.
Row 8: K1, p2, k3, p3, k8, p3, k3, p2, k1.
Row 9: P1, T3F, p2, T5F, p4, T5B, p2, T3B, p1.
Row 10: K2, p2, [k4, p3] twice, k4, p2, k2.
Row 11: P2, T3F, p3, T5F, T5B, p3, T3B, p2.
Row 12: K1, MB, k1, p2, k5, p6, k5, p2, k1, MB, k1.
Rows 1 to 12 form the pattern.

Reverse stocking st
Row 1: (RS) Purl.
Row 2: Knit.
Rows 1 to 2 form the pattern.

Body
Using 5 mm (size 8) needles or a circular needle cast on 244(268:292) sts. Work back and forth.
Row 1: (WS) * P4, k2; rep from * to last 4 sts, p4.
Row 2: (RS) * C2R, C2L, p2; rep from * to last 4 sts, C2R, C2L.
Row 3: * P4, k2; rep from * to last 4 sts, p4.
Rows 4–5: Repeat rows 2 and 3.
Row 6: (RS) Beginning all panels at 1st row unless otherwise stated and working a reverse st st background of 2 sts between each panel, work across the row as follows:
Panel 1, p2, Panel 2 starting at the 13th row, p2, * Panel 3, p2, Panel 4, p2, Panel 5A, p2, Panel 6, p2, Panel 7, p2, [Panel 1, p2] 0(1:2) times, Panel 8, [p2, Panel 1] 0(1:2) times, p2, Panel 7, p2, Panel 6, p2, Panel 5B, p2, Panel 4, p2, Panel 3 **, p2tog, p1, Panel 9, p1, p2tog; rep from * to **, p2, Panel

2 starting at 1st row, p2, Panel 1. 270(294:318) sts.
Row 6 sets the position of the panels and the reverse st st background.

Cont in pattern, remembering on every foll row to replace the decreases and p1 either side of panel 9 on row 6 with a 2 st reverse st st as with all other spacing in between cables, until body measures 19(19:19) cm [7½(7½: 7½) in], ending in a WS row. Weave in ends.

Shape armholes
Row 1: (RS) Patt 57 sts, cast off 26(38:50) sts while at the same time decreasing 2 of these sts across Panel 7 (one st on RHN after cast off), patt 103 sts, cast off 26(38:50) sts while at the same time decreasing 2 of these sts across Panel 7 (one st on RHN after cast off), patt 56 sts.
Turn and work on 57 sts for left front. Leave 104 sts for the back on a holder and leave 57 sts for right front on a second holder.

Left front
Cont on these 57 sts in cable panels on reverse st-st background as established and without shaping until left front measures 33(34:35) cm [13(13³⁄₈:13¾) in] from cast on edge, ending with a RS row.

Shape neck
Row 1: (WS) Patt 12 sts and leave on a holder, patt to end. 45 sts.
Row 2: Patt.

Row 3: Cast off 3 sts, patt to end. 42 sts.
Row 4: Patt.
Row 5: Cast off 2 sts, patt to end. 40 sts.
Row 6: Patt.
Rows 7–12: Work in pattern as established, dec 1 st at neck edge on every row. 34 sts.
Row 13: Patt.
Row 14: Work in patt, dec 2 sts at neck edge. 32 sts.
Row 15: Patt.
Row 16: Work in patt, dec 1 st at neck edge. 31 sts.
Row 17: Patt.
Row 18: Work in patt, dec 2 sts at neck edge. 29 sts.
Row 19: Patt.

Shape shoulder
Row 1: (RS) Cast off 8 sts, patt to end. 21 sts.
Row 2: Patt.
Row 3: Cast off 12 sts while at the same time dec 3 of these sts across Panel 5B, patt to end. 9 sts.
Row 4: Patt.
Cast off rem sts. Weave in ends.

Back
With WS facing, rejoin yarn to 104 sts left on holder for the back. Cont on these 104 sts in cable panels on reverse st-st background as established and without shaping until back measures 41(42:43) cm [16(16½:17) in] from cast on edge, ending with a WS row.

Shape shoulders
Rows 1–2: Cast off 8 sts at beg of row, patt to end. 88 sts.
Row 3: Cast off 12 sts at beg of row while at the same time dec 3 of these sts across Panel 5A, patt to end. 76 sts.
Row 4: Cast off 12 sts at beg of row while at the same time dec 3 of these sts across Panel 5B, patt to end. 64 sts.
Rows 5–6: Cast off 9 sts at beg of row, patt to end. 46 sts.
Leave sts on a holder.

Right front
With WS facing, rejoin yarn to 57 sts left on holder for right front. Cont on these 57 sts in cable panels on reverse st-st background as established and without shaping until right front measures 30(31:32) cm [12(12³⁄₈:12⁵⁄₈) in] from cast on edge, ending with a WS row. PM at both ends of last row.

Make buttonhole
Row 1: (RS) C2R, C2L, p1. Turn and work on these 5 sts only. Leave rem 52 sts on a holder.
Row 2: K1, p4.
Row 3: C2R, C2L, p1.
Rep rows 2 and 3 until work measures 5 cm (2 in) from row with marker 33(34:35) cm in [13(13¼:13¾)] from cast on edge, ending with a WS row. Do not break yarn. Leave these 5 sts on a holder.
With RS facing, join another ball of yarn to rem 52 sts left on a holder.

Cont in patt until work measures 5 cm (2 in) from row with marker 33(34:35) cm [13(13¼:13¾) in] from cast on edge, ending with a WS row. Break yarn.

Slip the 5 sts left on a holder back onto the needle holding the 52 sts. 57 sts on needle.

Shape neck

Row 1: (RS) [C2R, C2L, p2] twice and leave these 12 sts on a holder, patt to end. 45 sts.

Row 2: Patt.

Row 3: Cast off 3 sts, patt to end. 42 sts.

Row 4: Patt.

Row 5: Cast off 2 sts, patt to end. 40 sts.

Row 6: Patt.

Rows 7–12: Work in pattern as established, dec 1 st at neck edge on every row. 34 sts.

Row 13: Patt.

Row 14: Work in patt, dec 2 sts tog at neck edge. 32 sts.

Row 15: Patt.

Row 16: Work in patt, dec 1 st at neck edge. 31 sts.

Row 17: Patt.

Row 18: Work in patt, dec 2 sts tog at neck edge. 29 sts.

Row 19: Patt.

Shape shoulder

Row 1: (WS) Cast off 8 sts, patt to end. 21 sts.

Row 2: Patt.

Row 3: Cast off 12 sts while at the same time dec 3 of these sts across Panel 5B, patt to end. 9 sts.

Row 4: Patt.

Cast off rem sts.

Sleeves

Left
Using 5 mm (size 8) needles cast on 62(68:74) sts.
Row 1: (WS) K2, * p4, k2; rep from * to end.
Row 2: (RS) P2, * C2R, C2L, p2; rep from * to end.
Row 3: K2, * p4, k2; rep from * to end.
Rows 4–5: Repeat 2nd and 3rd rows.
Row 6: (RS) Beginning all panels at Row 1 unless otherwise stated and working a reverse stocking st background of 2 sts between each panel, work across the row as follows:
K2 (0:1), p2 (1:2), [Panel 1, p2] 0(1:1) times, Panel 3, p2, Panel 4, p2, Panel 7, p2, Panel 8, p2, Panel 3, p2, Panel 6, p2, Panel 7, p2, [Panel 1] 0(1:1) times, p2(1:2), k2(0:2). 70(76:82) sts.
Row 6 sets the position of the panels and the reverse st st background.
Cont in pattern as established, inc 1 st at each end of next 3rd and 17 foll 4th rows, bringing the extra sts into cabled rib pattern [Panel 1 separated by 2 sts reverse st-st]. 106(112:118) sts.
Cont in patt without shaping until sleeve measures 30 cm (12 in) ending with a WS row.
PM at both ends of last row.
Cont in patt as established until sleeve measures 35.5(38:40.5) cm [14(15:16) in], ending with a WS row.
Cast off all sts while at the same time dec 2 sts across Panel 3 and dec 2 sts across Panel 7.

Right
Using 5 mm (size 8) needles cast on 62(68:74) sts.
Row 1: (WS) K2, * p4, k2; rep from * to end.
Row 2: (RS) P2, * C2R, C2L, p2; rep from * to end.
Row 3: K2, * p4, k2; rep from * to end.
Rows 4–5: Repeat 2nd and 3rd rows.
Row 6: (RS) Beginning all panels at Row 1, unless otherwise stated, and working rev st-st of 2 sts between each panel, work across the row as follows:
K2(0:2), p2 (1:2), [Panel 1, p2] 0(1:1) times, Panel 7, p2, Panel 6, p2, Panel 3, p2, panel 8, p2, panel 7, p2, Panel 4, p2, Panel 3, p2, [Panel 1] 0(1:1) times, p2(1:2), k2(0:2). 70(76:82) sts.

The 6th row sets the position of the panels and the rev st-st background.
Cont in pattern as established, inc 1 st at both ends of 3rd and 17 foll 4th rows, bringing the extra sts into cabled rib pattern [Panel 1 separated by 2 sts reverse st st]. 106(112:118) sts.

Cont in patt without shaping until sleeve measures 30 cm (12 in), ending with a WS row. PM at each end of last row.

Cont in patt as established until sleeve measures 35.5(38:40.5) cm [14(15:16) in], ending with a WS row.
Cast off all sts while at the same time dec 2 sts across Panel 3 and dec 2 sts across Panel 7.

Neckband
Block the body, opening out the cables. Join shoulder seams using mattress st.

With RS facing, slip 12 sts left on a holder at right front neck onto a 5 mm (size 8) needle, pick up and knit 21 sts up right front neck. P2 then [C2R, C2L, p2] 7 times across remaining 44 sts of back while at the same time dec 2 sts across first Panel 3, inc 1 st at both ends of Panel 9 and then dec 2 sts across second panel 3, then pick up and knit 21 sts down left front neck, then [p2, C2R, C2L] twice across 12 sts left on a holder for left front neck. 118 sts.

Next row: (WS) * P4, k2; rep from * to last 4 sts, p4.
Next row: (RS) * C2R, C2L, p2; rep from * to last 4 sts, C2R, C2L.
Repeat last 2 rows once.
Cast off in patt.

Button
Using undyed, unspun fleece, felt a large spherical button as follows:

You will need detergent or soap for felting (dishwashing liquid will suffice) and hot water. The water needs to be hotter than tepid, but boiling water is not essential and risks scalding. Use rubber gloves to protect your hands from the drying effects of water and detergent.

It is best to felt in layers because this will cause the ball to become denser. Start with a small amount of fleece. Wet it with warm water and rub in a small amount of detergent. Roll the fleece in your hands as you would a ball of modelling clay, until you get a roughly shaped ball, then begin to add more pressure. Add more and more layers of fleece to the outside of the ball, wetting as you go, until you get a ball the desired size (approx 5 cm [2 in] in diameter). When the ball is in a rough sphere shape, continue to roll and rub it in between your hands, increasing pressure and dipping into hot water. To get the felt to really harden, submerge the ball alternately into hot and then cold water while continuously rubbing.

When the ball is the desired shape and size, leave to dry completely before attaching.

Assembly

Block the sleeves, opening out the cables.

Fold sleeves in half lengthwise. Matching the centrefold of the sleeve to the shoulder seam, join cast-off edge of sleeve to side edges of armholes using mattress st.

Join side edge of sleeve between sleeve cast-off edge and marker to cast-off edge at underarm using mattress st. (Join one sleeve side edge of sleeve to the underarm cast-off of the front and the other sleeve side edge to the cast-off of the back.) Join sleeve seams. The sleeve seam should match the centre of Panel 8 at the underarm.

Sew button to left front to correspond with buttonhole.

Enchanted woodland

Unlike a forest with its dense canopy, woodland allows sunlight to filter through the treetops. It is this beautiful, dappled light trickling through the leaves that creates the calming atmosphere of a woodland. This, and the sounds of birdsong, rustling leaves and snapping twigs, bring to mind autumnal shades of yellow, gold, brown and rust, fused with every shade of green – moss, fern, leaf, grass and more.

Contrasting textures

The textures found in a woodland are a mine of inspiration: springy moss, grainy bark, velvet petals, veiny leaves. The soft and hard contrast of bark and leaves is a great place to start.

There are many traditional patterns that use embossed leaves and petal shapes, and Aran patterns often include twining cables resembling bark and the twisted roots of trees. Just these two techniques combined in different ways can provide many varied fabrics. Ruffles and edgings can be layered to create leaf-like structures and individual leaf shapes can be knitted. Travelling ribs become the long, sturdy trunks of mythical sequoias, twining

1 Light falls through the canopy of leaves. **2** Ferns are an excellent representation of texture. **3** Rich autumnal colours. **4** Yarns wrap around crisp fading leaves. **5** Shades of green in a modular knitting pattern.

2

3

4

5

branches, or bark grain, and concentric circles echo the exposed age rings of a fallen oak.

All of these techniques can be utilized in many different fibres. Hard cotton or linen can represent the rough texture of bark, with silk mixes representing the luxurious sheen of leaves. Newly developed yarns made of plant and tree fibres, such as bark and paper, create uneven textures naturally. There are also synthetically developed fibres, such as viscose and rayon, that are derived from tree cellulose. Nettle is a superb example of a natural fibre spun from a staple of woodland plant life. It is versatile and seasonal, and with its hollow fibre it is incredibly warm and insulating. If spun tightly, the hollow core closes – making it great for summer wear, too.
-

6 A close-up of lines in tree bark. **7** Natural hand-dyed yarn is used here in an entrelac pattern. **8** Fall fruits create shape as well as colour. **9** Light and shade plays among these shadowy tree trunks. **10** Bright yellows appear in moderation in fruits, flowers, and lichens. **11** Fauna often mirror the palette of their environment in their colourings. **12** Raised knit and purl patterns in rust red. **13** Variegated yarn combines red and green tones. **14** Water can be an element of woodland, adding new textures, as well as reflecting woodland colours. **15** Mix colours of yarn together to create your own designs.

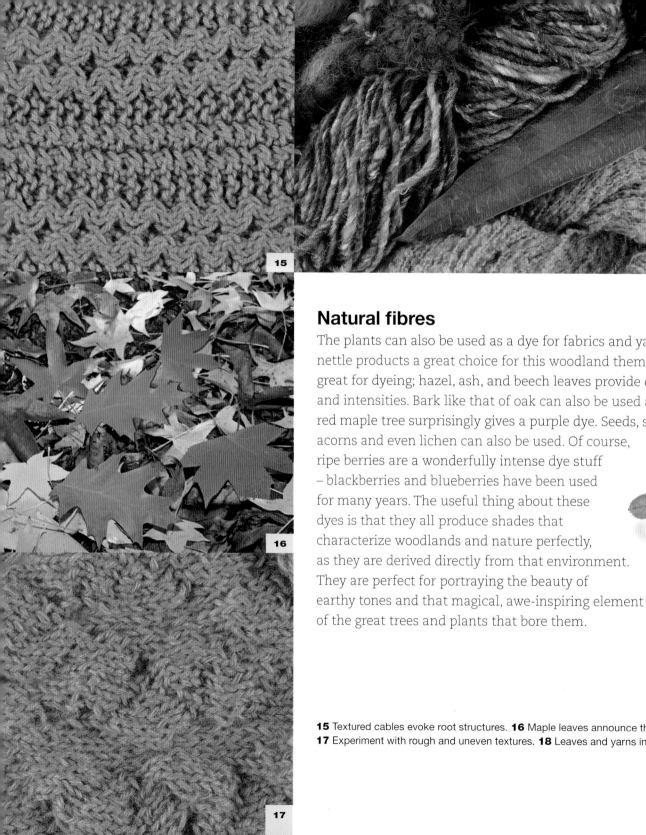

Natural fibres

The plants can also be used as a dye for fabrics and yarns, making nettle products a great choice for this woodland theme. Leaves are great for dyeing; hazel, ash, and beech leaves provide different colours and intensities. Bark like that of oak can also be used as dye, and the red maple tree surprisingly gives a purple dye. Seeds, such as acorns and even lichen can also be used. Of course, ripe berries are a wonderfully intense dye stuff – blackberries and blueberries have been used for many years. The useful thing about these dyes is that they all produce shades that characterize woodlands and nature perfectly, as they are derived directly from that environment. They are perfect for portraying the beauty of earthy tones and that magical, awe-inspiring element of the great trees and plants that bore them.

15 Textured cables evoke root structures. **16** Maple leaves announce the onset of autumn.
17 Experiment with rough and uneven textures. **18** Leaves and yarns intertwine.

Your Mood Board

Take a woodland walk for inspiration, and collect leaves and seed pods. Depending on the season, this will produce different results. Ready-mades that are created from the trees themselves, like wooden buttons, add to the effect.

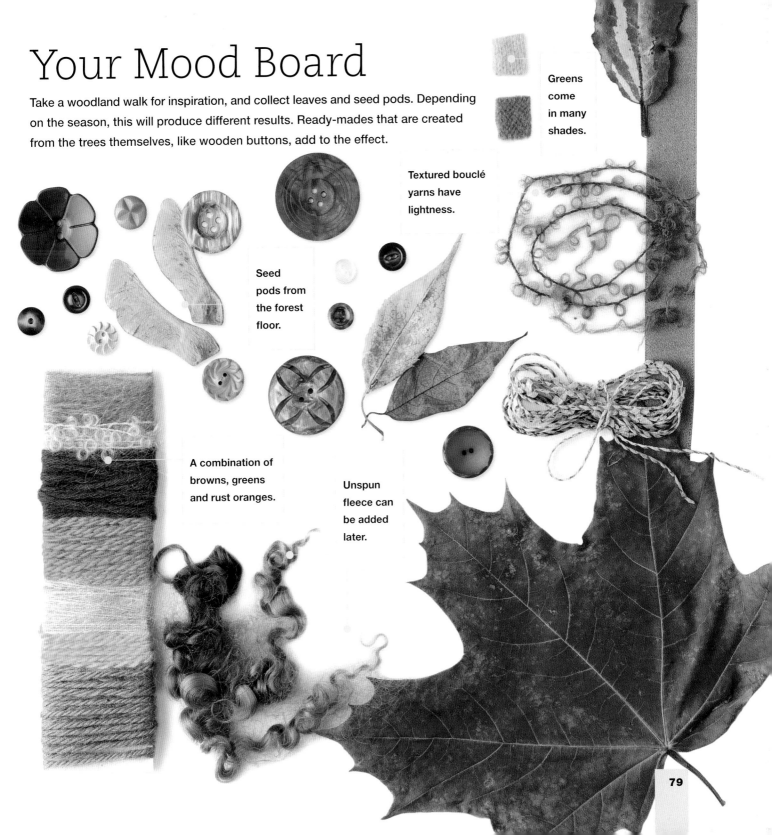

Greens come in many shades.

Textured bouclé yarns have lightness.

Seed pods from the forest floor.

A combination of browns, greens and rust oranges.

Unspun fleece can be added later.

Materials

- Short: Yarn A: 2 x Louisa Harding Grace, 50% silk, 50% wool, 50 g (1¾ oz), 110 m (120 yd) shade 09. Yarn B: 1 x Noro Ganpi Abaka Surabu, 40% ganpi abaka, 58% rayon, 2% nylon, 50 g (1¾ oz) 235 m (257 yd) shade 6

- 4 mm (size 6) needles

- Long: Yarn A: 2 x Blue Sky Alpacas worsted hand dyes 50% alpaca, 50% merino wool, 100 g (3½ oz), 91 m (100 yd) shade 2010 rusty orange Yarn B: 1 x Noro Ganpi Abaka Surabu, 40% ganpi abaka, 58% rayon, 2% nylon, 50 g (1¾ oz), 235 m (257 yd) shade 6. Yarn C: 1 x Frabjous Fibers nettle yarn, 100% nettle, 90 g (3 oz), 182 m (200 yd)

- 5 mm and 4 mm (size 8 and 6) needles

Measurements

Actual circumference

18	19	20.5	cm
7	7½	8	in

Length without ruffle: short version – 15.5 cm (6¼ in); long version 31 cm (12 in)

Gauge

Short: 38 sts to 10 cm (4 in) over bark cable patt on 4 mm (size 6) needles

Long: 28 sts to 10 cm (4 in) over cable patt on 5 mm (size 8) needles

Finn Fingerless Gloves

Noro's Ganpi Abaka is a yarn created from bark. Ganpi is a Japanese art paper made from fibres of eight-year-old trees growing in high-altitude mountains. These unusual and precious fibres produce a strong and lustrous paper. Abaka fibre derives from the stems of Manila hemp and is light and flexible. Noro has combined these fibres to create a yarn incorporating all of these qualities, resulting in a strong, lightweight, flexible yarn with a fantastic, lustrous yet subtle sheen. The delicate papery texture lends itself perfectly to representing the texture of leaves and bark. Consequently, this yarn is wonderful for use in a theme revolving around woodlands and nature. The greens and yellows of the shade chosen are reminiscent of foliage and combined with the rustling papery texture; the subtle suggestion of leaves on a branch works well in this pattern.

The pattern is shown in two lengths and colours. Wear the short pair to keep your wrists warm when your fingers need to be free to work. The long pair can be worn under a cropped-sleeve jacket to keep the whole lower arm snug.

Yarn alternatives: Keep the main yarn as smooth and simple as possible to allow the cabled pattern to stand out. For the ruffle, experiment with other DK fancy yarns.

Special abbreviations

C6F – Cable 6 front. Slip next 3 sts onto a cable needle and hold at front of work, [k2, p1] from left hand needle, then [p1, k2] from cable needle.

C6B – Cable 6 back. Slip next 3 sts onto a cable needle and hold at back of work, [k2, p1] from left hand needle then [p1, k2] from cable needle.

K1/MB – Either k1 stitch or make a bobble. Bobbles are made randomly as the back of the glove is worked. Make bobble as follows [K1, p1, k1] all into next stitch, turn and k3, turn and p3, turn and k3, turn and purl the 3 sts tog. Bobble completed.

Short version

Back (both alike)

Using 4 mm (size 6) needles and Yarn A cast on 38(38:38) sts.
Row 1: P2, [k4, p2] 6 times.
Row 2: K2, [p4, k2] 6 times.
Row 3: P1, [C6F] 6 times, p1.
Row 4: K1, p2, [k2, p4] 5 times, k2, p2, k1.
Row 5: P1, k2, [p2, k1, k1/MB, k2] 5 times, p2, k2, p1.
Row 6: K1, p2, [k2, p4] 5 times, k2, p2, k1.
Row 7: P1, k2, [p2, k2, k1/MB, k1] 5 times, p2, k2, p1.
Row 8: K1, p2, [k2, p4] 5 times, k2, p2, k1.
Row 9: P2, k2, [C6B] 5 times, k2, p2.
Row 10: K2, [p4, k2] 6 times.
Row 11: P2, [k4, p2] 6 times.
Row 12: K2, [p4, k2] 6 times.
Row 13: P2, [k4, p2] 6 times.
Row 14: K2, [p4, k2] 6 times.
3rd to 14th rows form the patt.
Rows 15–50: Rep rows 3 to 14, 3 times.

Rows 51–54: Rep rows 3 to 6 once. Cast off, while at the same time, working the 7th row of the patt.

Palm
Right-hand glove
With RS of back of glove facing, using 4 mm (size 6) needles and Yarn A and starting at cast-on edge, pick up and k35(35:35) sts along side edge of back of glove. Cast off knitwise.

Left-hand glove
With RS of back of glove facing, using 4 mm (size 6) needles and Yarn A and starting at cast-off edge, pick up and k35(35:35) sts along side edge of back of glove.

Cont in g st until front of glove measures 7.5(9:10) cm [3(3½:4) in] ending with a WS row. Cast off knitwise.

Ruffled edging
Top of left glove
With RS facing, using 4 mm (size 6) needles and Yarn B, pick up and k38 sts across cast-off edge of the back of the glove, including the join where the sts were picked up for the front, then pick up and k1 st between each garter st ridge, and then pick up and k1 st on the garter st cast-off row.
Row 1: (WS) Purl.
Row 2: [K1, yo, k1] into every st.
Row 3: Purl.
Row 4: Cast off knitwise.
Bottom of left glove

With RS facing, using 4 mm (size 6) needles and Yarn B, pick up and k1 st on the garter st cast off row, then pick up and k1 st between every garter st ridge, inc the join where the sts were picked up for the front, and then pick up and k38 sts across cast-on edge of the back of the glove.
Row 1: (WS) Purl.
Row 2: [K1, yo, k1] into every st.
Row 3: Purl.
Row 4: Cast off, while at the same time, working twice (as k1 into the front of the st, then k1 into the back of the st) into every st across the row.

Top of right glove
With RS facing, using 4 mm (size 6) needles and Yarn B, pick up and k1 st on the garter st cast-off row, then pick up and k1 st between every garter st ridge, including the join where the sts were picked up for the front, and then pick up and k38 sts across cast off edge of the back of the glove.
Row 1: (WS) Purl.
Row 2: [K1, yo, k1] into every st.
Row 3: Purl.
Row 4: Cast off knitwise.

Bottom of right glove
With RS facing, using 4 mm (size 6) needles and Yarn B, pick up and k38 sts across cast-on edge of the back of the glove, including the join where the sts were picked up for the front, then pick up and k1 st between each g st ridge, and then pick up and k1 st on the g st cast-off row.
Row 1: (WS) Purl.

Row 2: [K1, yo, k1] into every st.
Row 3: Purl.
Row 4: Cast off while at the same time working twice (as k1 into the front of the st then k1 into the back of the st) into every st across the row.

Make up
Join seam, leaving 5 cm (2 in) of seam open for thumb, 5 cm (2 in) from top of glove.

Long version
For this version the cabled section is without bobbles, but these can be added at intervals, if desired, as for the short version.

Back (both alike)
Using 5 mm (size 8) needles and Yarn A, cast on 26(26:26)sts.
Row 1: P2, [k4, p2] to end of row.
Row 2: K2, [p4, k2] to end of row.
Row 3: P1, [C6F] to last st, p1.
Row 4: K1, p2, [k2, p4] to last 5 sts, k2, p2, k1.
Row 5: P1, k2, [p2, k1, k1/MB, k2] to last 5 sts, p2, k2, p1.
Row 6: K1, p2, [k2, p4] to last 5 sts, k2, p2, k1.
Row 7: P1, k2, [p2, k2, k1/MB, k1] to last 5 sts, p2, k2, p1.
Row 8: K1, p2, [k2, p4] to last 5 sts, k2, p2, k1.
Row 9: P2, k2, [C6B] to last 4 sts, k2, p2.
Row 10: K2, [p4, k2] to end of row.
Row 11: P2, [k4, p2] to end of row.
Rep last 2 rows once more.
Row 14: K2, [p4, k2] to end of row.
Rows 3–14 form the patt.

Rep these 12 rows twice more.
Next row: *P2, k2, rep from * to last 2 sts, p2. Rep last row until glove measures 31 cm (12 in), cast off all sts.

Palm
Using Yarn A, cast on 15(18:21) sts, and knit 13 cm (5 in) even in garter st.

Next row: *K2, inc 1, rep from * to end of row (20,24,28 sts).
Next row: *K2, p2, rep from * to end of row. Cont in 2 x 2 rib until glove measures 31 cm (12 in) cast off all sts.

Ruffled edge (both alike)
Sew left seam. Using 4 mm (size 6) needles and Yarn B, pick up and k40 sts along top edge of glove.
Next row: Purl.
Next row: [K1, yo, k1] into every st.
Next row: Purl.
Cast off all sts. Using 4 mm (size 6) needles and Yarn C, pick up and k40 sts along 1 row below last frill.
Next row: Purl.
Next row: [K1, yo, k1] into every st.
Next row: Purl.
Cast off all sts. Sew up rem seam, leaving a 4 cm (1½ in) gap for thumb, 4 cm (1½ in) from top of glove.

Materials

- **House of Hemp Expressions, hand-coloured 100% hemp yarn, 50 g (1¾ oz), 85 m (93 yd)**
  Yarn A: 2 x Dah, Yarn B: 1 x Yippi, Yarn C : 1 x Ah, Yarn D: 1 x Alchemy silken straw 40 g (1½ oz) 216 m (236 yd) in fauna

- **Set of four 4 mm (size 6) dpn**

- **4 mm (size 6) circular needle 40 cm (16 in) long (optional)**

- **Wide satin ribbon to wrap around crown (optional)**

Measurements

To fit an average size head

56 cm (22 in)

Actual size all around 49 cm (19⅜ in)

Tension

26 sts and 44 rows to 10 cm (4 in) square over patt on 4 mm (size 6) needles, or the size required to give the correct tension.

Note: Yarn quantities are based on average requirements and are therefore approximate. Yarn alternatives: any DK or worsted yarn.

Henna Sun Hat

This hat is knitted from a hemp yarn, which is derived directly from a plant, affording the yarn its tough, stiff qualities that make it great for the summer. When knitted, the hemp resembles a traditional straw hat and keeps its shape the same way. This particular stitch looks more like a woven fabric than a knitted one. Hemp is now available in many beautifully subtle and springlike shades, offering you more choices than in the usual straw yellow or brown palettes.

The brim is knitted so that the natural roll of the fabric curls upwards, aiding the rigidity of the brim and lending the perfect platform to layer plentiful blooms around it, whether real or fake. A large bow can be used to cover up the change in colour between the brim and crown sections, creating a dramatic look. A bonnet is a symbol of spring and the wildflowers of the countryside, so put a flower in your hat and enjoy being outside in the warm weather.

Hat

Worked as one-piece starting at the brim.

Using a set of four 4 mm (size 6) dpn or a 4 mm (size 6) circular needle and Yarn A, cast on 256 sts. Distribute the stitches over the dpns in multiples of 2 and position the needles for working in the round. PM at beginning of the round and slip the marker at the beginning of every round.

The stitch patt gives a k1 at the end of odd-numbered rounds followed by a k1 at the beginning of the next (even-numbered) round, and also a sl 1 wyif at the end of even-numbered rounds followed by a sl 1 wyif at the beginning of the next (odd-numbered) round. When changing from an odd- to an even-numbered round, pull the yarn firmly at the front of the work.

Rnd 1: (RS) * Sl 1 wyif, k1; rep from * to end.
Rnd 2: (RS) * K1, sl 1 wyif; rep from * to end.
Rnds 3–10: Rep 1st and 2nd rounds 4 times.
Rnd 11: (dec round) * [Sl 1 wyif, k1] 3 times, sl 1 wyif, yarn to back, k2tog, psso, [k1, sl 1 wyif] 3 times, k1; rep from * 15 times more. 224 sts.

Work 10 rounds in patt.

Rnd 22: * K1, [sl 1 wyif, k1] twice, sl 1 wyif, yarn to back, k2tog, psso, [k1, sl 1 wyif] 3 times. Rep from * 15 times more. 192 sts.

Work 10 rnds in patt.

Rnd 33: * [Sl 1 wyif, k1] twice, sl 1 wyif, yarn to back, k2tog, psso, [k1, sl 1 wyif] twice, k1; rep from * 15 times more. 160 sts.

Work 10 rounds in patt.

Rnd 44: * K1, sl 1 wyif, k1, sl 1 wyif, yarn to back, k2tog, psso, [k1, sl 1 wyif] twice. Rep from * 15 times more. 128 sts. Brim completed. Break Yarn A.

Side of hat

Turn work inside out so that the WS is now the RS. If using a circular needle, change to a set of four 4 mm (size 6) dpn. Join Yarn B.

Rnd 1: (RS) * Sl 1 wyif, k1; rep from * to end.
Rnd 2: (RS) * K1, sl 1 wyif; rep from * to end.
Rnds 3–42: Rep 1st and 2nd rounds 20 times.
Rnd 43: * Sl 1 wyif, k1; rep from * to end.

Shape crown

Rnd 1: [K1, sl 1 wyif] 3 times, sl 1 wyib, k2tog, psso, * [sl 1 wyif, k1] 3 times, sl 1 wyif, sl 1 wyib, k2tog, psso; rep from * 5 times more, [sl 1 wyif, k1] 3 times, sl 1 wyif, k2tog, psso, * k1, sl 1 wyif] 3 times, k1, sl 1 wyif, k2tog, psso; rep from * 4 times more. 102 sts.

Work 5 rnds in patt.

Rnd 7: [K1, sl 1 wyif] twice, sl 1 wyib, k2tog, psso, * [sl 1 wyif, k1] twice, sl 1 wyif, sl 1 wyib, k2tog, psso; rep from * 5 times more, [sl 1 wyif, k1] twice, sl 1 wyif, k2tog, psso, * [k1, sl 1 wyif] twice, k1, sl 1 wyif, k2tog, psso; rep from * 4 times more. 76 sts.

Work 5 rnds in patt.

Rnd 13: K1, sl 1 wyif, sl 1 wyib, k2tog, psso, * sl 1 wyif, k1, sl 1 wyif, sl 1 wyib, k2tog, psso; rep from * 5 times, sl 1 wyif, k1, sl 1 wyif, k2tog, psso, * k1, sl 1 wyif, k1, sl 1 wyif, k2tog, psso; rep from * 4 times more. 50 sts.

Work 5 rnds in patt.

Rnd 19: Sl 1 wyib, k2tog, psso, *sl 1 wyif, sl 1 wyib, k2tog, psso; rep from * 5 times, sl 1 wyif, k2tog, psso, * k1, sl 1 wyif, k2tog, psso; rep from * 4 times more. 24 sts.

Work 5 rnds in patt.

Rnd 25: [k2tog] 12 times. 12 sts.

Break yarn, thread through rem sts and pull firmly to gather. Fasten off and weave in ends.

Add a ribbon around the crown of the hat, if desired. A shiny ribbon may need a slip stitch to keep it in place.

Materials

- Approx 350(400:450) g [12¼(14:15¾) oz] 976 (1,115:1255) yd (893:1020:1148 m) (Hawthorne Heritage Crafts semi-worsted Whitefaced Woodland yarn, naturally dyed in varying shades of hazel leaves

- 3.25 mm (size 3) and 3.75 mm (size 5) needles

- Set of four or five 3.25 mm (size 3) dpn or a 3.25 mm (size 3) 30-cm (12-in) long circular needle

- Stitch holders

- 2 or 3 small buttons

Measurements

To fit bust

81–86	91–97	102–107	cm
32–34	36–38	40–42	in

Actual size

89.5	100	110.5	cm
35	39½	43½	in

Length to shoulder

45	46	47	cm
17½	18	18½	in

Sleeve seam
10 cm (4 in)

Tension

23 sts and 30 rows to 10 cm (4 in) square over st st on 3.75 mm (size 5) needles

Spruce Sweater

This sweater was designed around this beautiful handspun yarn. It is spun from a woodland breed of fleece and is naturally dyed by hazel leaves in many differing shades of soft green. The delicate traditional shape and pattern of the sweater with leaf motif beautifully displays this wonderful yarn. However, that is not to say that any wool or other fibres could not also reproduce the beauty captured here. You can transform the design by using brighter, more autumnal colours or by using contrasting colours in the ruffles or yoke.

The vertical arrangement of the panels and leaf motifs give the top a firm, strong base, reminiscent of tree trunks, while the lacy embellishment is meant to represent foliage. The idea of having about seven different intensities of the same dye lot makes one think of how the light filters through the trees to give a dappled, pretty colour palette. Here, the yarn has been alternately used by striping up every two rows or so, but you could also grade the colour by using larger stripes, causing the colour to look more diffused from light to dark. Of course, just one, all-over shade could also be used to great effect.

Yarn alternatives: Any DK or roughly sportweight yarn. Yarn quantities are based on average requirements and are therefore approximate.

Figures in parentheses ( ) refer to larger sizes. When only one set of figures is given, it applies to all sizes.

Special abbreviation
P2sso – pass two slip stitches over.

Stitch patterns
Panel 1
5 sts, 4 rows.
Row 1: (RS) K5.
Row 2: P5.
Row 3: K2tog, yo, k1, yo, ssk.
Row 4: P5.
Rows 1 to 4 form the pattern.

Panel 2 (Smaller leaf)
The number of stitches incs and then decs over the rows.
Row 1: (RS) P1.
Row 2: K1.
Row 3: M1k, k1, m1k.
Row 4: P3.
Row 5: K1, yo, k1, yo, k1.
Row 6: P5.
Row 7: K2, yo, k1, yo, k2.
Row 8: P7.
Row 9: K2, slip next 2 sts knitwise onto RHN, k1, p2sso, k2.
Row 10: P5.
Row 11: K1, slip next 2 sts knitwise onto RHN, k1, p2sso, k1.
Row 12: P3.
Row 13: Slip next 2 sts knitwise onto RHN, k1, p2sso.
Row 14: K1.
Row 15: P1.
Row 16: K1.
Rows 1 to 16 form the patt.
Work a total of 8 patt reps on the front of the sweater. After the 8th patt rep has been worked cont this panel as rev stocking stitch.

Panel 3 (Larger leaf)
The number of stitches incs and then decs over the rows.
Row 1: (RS) On the first patt rep, m1p. On the second and third patt rep, p1.
Row 2: K1.
Row 3: Yo, k1, yo.
Row 4: P3.
Row 5: K1, yo, k1, yo, k1.
Row 6: P5.
Row 7: K2, yo, k1, yo, k2.
Row 8: P7.
Row 9: K3, yo, k1, yo, k3.
Row 10: P9.
Row 11: Sl 1, k1, psso, k5, k2tog.
Row 12: P7.
Row 13: Sl 1, k1, psso, k3, k2tog.
Row 14: P5.
Row 15: Sl 1, k1, psso, k1, k2tog.
Row 16: P3.
Row 17: Sl 1, k2tog, psso.
Row 18: K1.
Row 19: P1.
Row 20: K1.
Rows 1 to 20 forms the patt. There are 3 patt reps in all (60 rows) on the front. This panel stops at the start of the V-neck.

Back
Using 3.25 mm (size 3) needles, cast on 78(90:102) sts.
Row 1: (RS) *K2, p2; rep from * to last 2 sts, k2.
Row 2: P2, * k2, p2; rep from * to end.
Rows 1 and 2 form 2 x 2 rib. Cont in 2 x 2 rib until back measures 10 cm (4 in), ending with a WS row. Change to 3.75 mm (size 5) needles.
Row 1: (RS) P39(45:51), m1p, p39(45:51). 79(91:103) sts.
Row 2: (WS) Knit.
Cont in rev st–st for 58 more rows, inc 1 st at beach end of the 2nd row of these 58 rows and on 11 foll 4th rows. 103(115:127) sts.

Shape armholes
Cast off 4(5:6) sts at beg of next 2 rows. 95(105:115) sts.
Cont in rev st-st for 58(62:64) rows, while at the same time, dec 1 st at each end of the next 3(5:7) rows and then on the 4(4:5) foll alt rows. 81(87:91) sts.

Shape shoulders
Cast off 7(7:7) sts at beg of next 2 rows. 67(73:77) sts.
Cast off 7(7:8) sts at beg of next 2 rows. 53(59:61) sts.
Cast off 7(8:8) sts at beg of next 2 rows. 39(43:45) sts.
Leave rem sts on a holder for back neck.

Front
Using 3.25 mm (size 3) needles cast on 78(90:102) sts.
Row 1: (RS) K2, p2; rep from * to last 2 sts, k2.
Row 2: (WS) P2, * k2, p2; rep from * to end.

Cont in 2 x 2 rib until front measures

10 cm (4 in), ending with a WS row. Change to 3.75 mm (size 5) needles. The number of stitches for Panels 2 and 3 are each counted as 1 st in the counts given in the patt. When counting stitches, make an allowance for the changing number of stitches in Panels 2 and 3.

Row 1: (RS) P1(7:13), work first row of Panel 1, p9, work first row of Panel 2, p9, work first row of Panel 1, p9, work first row of Panel 3, p9, work first row of Panel 1, p9, work first row of Panel 2, p9, work first row of Panel 1, p1(7:13). 79(91:103) sts.

Row 2: K1(7:13), work 2nd row of Panel 1, k9, work 2nd row of Panel 2, k9, work 2nd row of Panel 1, k9, work 2nd row of Panel 3, k9, work 2nd row of Panel 1, k9, work 2nd row of Panel 2, k9, work 2nd row of Panel 1, k1(7:13).

Cont in panels as est on rev st-st background for 58 more rows, inc 1 st at each end of the 2nd row of and then on 11 foll 4th rows. 103(115:127) sts. Panel 3 is now completed.

Shape armholes and V-neck

Row 1: (RS) Cast off 4(5:6) sts at beg of row (1 stitch on RHN), patt 46(51:56). 47(52:57) sts on RHN. Leave rem 52(58:64) sts on a holder for RS of neck.

Row 2: (WS) Patt.
Cont in patt for 58(62:64) rows, while at the same time, dec 1 st at armhole edge on next 3(5:7) rows, and then on 4(4:5) foll alt rows,

and also at the same time dec 1 st at neck edge on the next row and 2(4:6) foll alt rows and then on 16(16:15) foll 3rd rows. 21(22:23) sts.

Shape shoulder

Row 1: (RS) Cast off 7(7:7) sts, patt to end. 14(15:16) sts.
Row 2: (WS) Patt.
Row 3: Cast off 7(7:8) sts, patt to end. 7(8:8) sts.
Row 4: Patt.
Cast off rem sts purlwise.

With RS facing, rejoin yarn to 52(58:64) sts on a holder for right side of neck. Slip centre front st onto a holder, patt to end. 51(57:63) sts. Complete to match left side of front neck, rev shaping.

Yoke

Using 3.75 mm (size 5) needles, cast on 3 sts.
Row 1: (RS) Purl.
Row 2: (WS) Knit.
Cont in rev st-st, inc 1 st at each end of next row and 2(4:6), foll alt rows and then on 9(9:9) foll 3rd rows. 27(31:35) sts.
Work 2(2:0) rows without shaping.
Next row: (RS) P8(10:12), while at the same time, inc 1(1:0) st at beg of the row. 9(11:12) sts on RHN. Turn and work on these sts only. Leave rem 19(21:23) sts on a holder for right side. Cont in rev st-st, inc 1 st on every 3rd row from the previous inc at side edge 7(7:7) times more while at the same time dec 1 st at neck edge on

next 6(10:12) rows and then on 8(6:5) foll alt rows. 2 sts.
K1 row.
Cast off purlwise.

Return to 19(21:23) sts left on a holder for right side of yoke.
With RS facing, slip 11 sts onto a holder for centre front neck, purl to end. Complete to match left side of yoke, reversing shapings.

Sleeves (both alike)
Using 3.25 mm (size 3) needles, cast on 70(74:82) sts.
Work in 2 x 2 rib for 5 cm (2 in) as given for the back.
Change to 3.75 mm (size 5) needles.
Row 1: (RS) P19(21:25), work first row of Panel 1, p9, k2, m1k, k2, p9, work first row of Panel 1, p19(21:25). 71(75:83) sts.
Row 2: (WS) K19(21:25), [work row 2 of Panel 1, k9] twice, work row 2 of Panel 1, k19(21:25).
Row 3: (RS) P19(21:25), [work row 3 of Panel 1, p9] twice, work row 3 of Panel 1, p19(21:25).
Row 4: K19(21:25), [work row 4 of Panel 1, k9] twice, work row 4 of Panel 1, k19(21:25).
Row 5: (RS) P19(21:25), [work row 1 of Panel 1, p9] twice, work row 1 of Panel 1, p19(21:25). Cont in patt as est without inc, until sleeve measures 10 cm (4 in) ending with a WS row.

Shape sleeve top
Cast off 4(5:6) sts at beg of next 2 rows. 63(65:71) sts.
Cont in patt for 24(26:40) rows, dec 1 st at each end of the first of these rows and then on every foll alt row. 39(39:31) sts.
Cont in patt for 22(22:10) rows, dec 1 st at both ends of the first of these rows and then on every foll 3rd row. 23(23:23) sts.
Cast off in patt. PM between the 6th and 7th to last rows before the cast-off. Block each piece.

Neck ruffle
With RS of front facing, using 3.75 mm (size 5) needle, pick up and k50(52:54) sts down left side of V neck, k1 stitch at centre front, then pick up and k50(52:54) sts up right side of V neck. 101(105:109) sts.
Row 1: (WS) Purl.
Row 2: [K1, yo, k1] into every stitch.
Row 3: Purl.
Row 4: Cast off, while at the same time working twice in each stitch (as k1 into the front of the stitch then k1 into the back of the stitch) across the row.

Shoulder ruffles (both alike)
Join shoulder seams.
With RS facing, using 3.75 mm (size 5) needles, pick up and k44(47:49) sts from underarm to shoulder seam, 1 st at the seam and then 44(47:49) sts from shoulder to underarm. 89(95:99) sts. Complete as given for the neck ruffle.

Neckband
Join yoke to centre front, making sure that the neck ruffle remains on the RS of the garment.
Using a set of four or five 3.25 mm (size 3) dpn or a 3.25 mm (size 3) circular needle, starting at left shoulder, pick up and k28(32:36) sts down left side of front neck, working through the ruffle and the V-neck edges, until the yoke is reached and then working through the neck edge of the yoke only, [k2, p2] across 11 sts for centre front, while at the same time, inc 1 stitch, pick up and k28(32:36) sts up right side of front neck, then [k2, p2] across 39(43:45) sts for back neck, while at the same time inc (inc:dec) 1 stitch. 108(120:128) sts.
PM for beginning of round.
1st round: * K2, p2; rep from * to end.
Cont in 2 x 2 rib as est until neckband measures 4 cm (1½ in).
Cast off all sts. Weave in ends.

Assembly
Insert a gathering thread between the markers at the top of the sleeve and evenly gather. Fold sleeve in half lengthwise and, with centre fold against the shoulder seam, sew the sleeve into place.

Join side and sleeve seams. Sew buttons down centre front of yoke.

Materials

- Yarn A: 2 x 25 g (1 oz) GGH Soft Kid, 70% super kid mohair, 5% wool, 25% polyamide, 138 m (151 yd), shade 006 – brown
  Yarn B: 2 x 14 g (½ oz) balls Habu A-126 mohair lp kusaki-zome, 81% mohair, 9% wool, 10% nylon, 55 m (62 yd), 23 Rosemary – light green bouclé. Yarn C: 2 x 14 g (½ oz) balls Habu A-123 mohair lp, 81% mohair, 9% wool, 10% nylon, 55 m (62 yd), 44 Dark brown bouclé
  Yarn D: 2 x 14 g (½ oz) balls Habu A-32B silk mohair kusa, 60% silk, 40% mohair, 167 m (186 yd), 23 Rosemary – light green
  Yarn E: 1 x 14 g (½ oz) ball Habu A-126 mohair lp kusaki-zome, 81% mohair, 9% wool, 10% nylon, 55 m (62 yd), 22 Gobaishi – medium green bouclé
  Yarn F: 1 x GGH Bel Air, 90% merino extra-fine, 10% polyamide, 50 g (1¾ oz), 130 m (142 yd), shade 11

- 45–50 cm (18–20 in) of smooth waste yarn

- 4 and 6 mm (sizes 6 and 10) needles 4 mm (size 6) circular needle 60–80 cm (24–32 in) long (optional)
  One size 7 mm (10½) needle

- Size 6 mm (J-10) crochet hook

Measurements

Length along straight edge including depth of edging: approx 160 cm (63 in). Exact tension is not a requirement.

Sequoia Shawl

This design moves away from the traditional rectangular- or triangular-shaped shawls and wraps. It was inspired by nature and organic shaping, looking towards the mighty woodland trees. The occasional felled tree and resulting exposed rings in the stump provided the perfect ideas.

This wrap is semicircular in construction, with subtle stripes reflecting those concentric circles. The softness of the slowly curving shape is incredibly pretty, and the subtly differing tones in each 'age ring' create a delicate and harmonious palette. The knitting is straightforward, with only a few lace holes to maintain the delicate look. You can even thread ends of yarn without knitting along a curved stripe for added, unusual texture.

The yarns are soft and lightweight mohair and alpaca fibres, which are also quite fluffy and ethereal, perfect for representing the magical qualities of the light and shade in woodland. The odd stripe of bouclé mohair emphasizes the spongy, cosy texture inspired by ground and bark mosses. The colours stick faithfully to mosses, wood and bark to recreate a woodland feel. However, a far bolder, brighter look can be achieved with stronger colours and a greater contrast within the colours you choose.

Yarn alternatives: Any lace-weight mohairs or other fibres, or try other 4-ply and DK mohairs. Try to keep the fibres and yarns lightweight to retain the ethereal beauty of the shawl.

Shawl

Start at the centre of the straight edge. Using 6 mm (size 10) needles and waste yarn, cast on 6 sts.

Rows 1–2: Knit.

Break waste yarn.

Joining, dropping and breaking yarns as necessary, and changing to a circular needle, if desired, work back and forth in rows as follows:

Row 1: (WS) Leaving a long tail, and using Yarn A knit. Thread the tail through the 6 sts on the needle.

Row 2: (Inc row) (RS) Using A, k1, [k1, yo] 3 times, k2. 9 sts.

Rows 3–4: Using Yarn A, k. 9 sts.

Row 5: Using A, k. 9 sts.

Row 6: (Inc row) Using B, k1, [k1, yo] 6 times, k2. 15 sts.

Rows 7–9: Using B, k. 15 sts.

Rows 10–11: Using C, k. 15 sts.

Row 12: (Inc row) Using D, k1, [k1, yo] 12 times, k2. 27 sts.

Rows 13–15: Using D, k. 27 sts.

Row 16: Using E, k2, [yo, k2tog] 12 times, k1. 27 sts.

Row 17: Using E, k. 27 sts.

Rows 18–19: Using B, k. 27 sts.

Row 20: (Inc row) Using B, k2, [yo, k2] 12 times, k1. 39 sts.

Row 21: Using B, k. 39 sts.

Rows 22–23: Using E, k. 39 sts.

Row 24: Using A, k2, [yo, k2tog, k1] 12 times, k1. 39 sts.

Row 25: Using A, k. 39 sts.

Row 26: (Inc row) Using A, k1, [k3, yo] 12 times, k2. 51 sts.

Row 27: Using A, k. 51 sts.

Rows 28–29: Using C, k. 51 sts.

Row 30: Using D, k1, [k2, k2tog, yo] 12 times, k2. 51 sts.

Row 31: Using D, k. 51 sts.

Row 32: (Inc row) Using D, k2, [yo, k4] 12 times, k1. 63 sts.

Row 33: Using D, k. 63 sts.

Row 34: Using B, k1, [k3, k2tog, yo] 12 times, k2. 63 sts.

Row 35: Using B, k. 63 sts.

Rows 36–37: Using E, k. 63 sts.

Row 38: (Inc row) Using D, k1, [k5, yo] 12 times, k2. 75 sts.

Row 39: Using D, k. 75 sts.

Rows 40–41: Using C, k. 75 sts.

Rows 42–43: Using B, k. 75 sts.

Row 44: (Inc row) Using A, k2, [yo, k2, yo, k2tog, k2] 12 times, k1. 87 sts.

Row 45: Using A, k. 87 sts.

Rows 46–47: Using E, k. 87 sts.

Rows 48–49: Using D, k. 87 sts.

Row 50: (Inc row) Using D, k1, [k1, k2tog, yo, k4, yo] 12 times, k2. 99 sts.

Row 51: Using D, k. 99 sts.

Row 52: Using A, k. 99 sts.

Row 53: Using A, k1, [k1, wind around tip of RHN twice] 97 times, k1. 99 sts.

Row 54: Using B, k1, [k1 drop extra lp from LHN] 97 times, k1. 99 sts.

Row 55: Using B, k. 99 sts.

Row 56: (Inc row) Using B, k2, [yo, k3, yo, k2tog, k3] 12 times, k1. 111 sts.

Row 57: Using B, k. 111 sts.

Rows 58–59: Using E, k. 111 sts.

Row 60: Using C, k10, [yo, k2tog, k8] 10 times, k1. 111 sts.

Row 61: Using C, k. 111 sts.

Row 62: (Inc row) Using D, k1, [k4, yo, k2tog, k3, yo] 12 times, k2. 123 sts.

Row 63: Using D, k. 123 sts.

Row 64: Using D, k1, [k1, wind yarn around tip of RHN twice] 121 times, k1. 123 sts. PM at both ends of row.

Row 65: Using D, k1, [k1 drop extra lp from LHN] 121 times, k1. 123 sts.

Rows 66–67: Using E, k. 123 sts.

Row 68: (Inc row) Using A, k2, [yo, k3, yo, k2tog, yo, k2tog, k3] 12 times, k1. 135 sts.

Row 69: Using A, k. 135 sts.

Rows 70–71: Using B, k. 135 sts.

Rows 72–73: Using C, k. 135 sts.

Row 74: (Inc row) Using B, k2, [[yo, k2tog] 5 times, yo, k1] 12 times, k1. 147 sts.

Row 75: Using B, k. 147 sts.

Rows 76–77: Using D, k. 147 sts.

Row 78: Using A, k2, [yo, k2tog] 72 times, k1. 147 sts.

Row 79: Using A, k. 147 sts.

Row 80: (Inc row) Using D, k1, [yo, k6, yo, k2tog, k4] 12 times, k2. 159 sts.

Row 81: Using D, purl. 159 sts.

Rows 82–83: Using C, k. 159 sts.

Row 84: Using B, k1, [k1, winding yarn around tip of RHN twice] 157 times, k1. 159 sts.

Row 85: Using B, k1, [k1 drop extra lp from LHN] 157 times, k1. 159 sts.

Row 86: (Inc row) Using D, k2, [yo, k6, yo, k2tog, k5] 12 times, k1. 171 sts.

Row 87: Using D, k. 171 sts.

Row 88: Using A, k1, [k5, k2tog, yo] 24 times, k2. 171 sts.

Row 89: Using A, k. 171 sts.

Rows 90–91: Using E, k.

Row 92: (Inc row) Using C, k1, [[k3, k2tog, yo] twice, k4, yo] 12 times, k2. 183 sts.

Row 93: Using C, k. 183 sts.

Rows 94–95: Using D, k. 183 sts.

Row 96: Using E, k1, [k1, winding yarn around tip of RHN twice] 181 times, k1. 183 sts.

Row 97: Using E, k1, [k1 dropping extra lp from LHN] 181 times, k1. 183 sts.

Row 98: (Inc row) Using B, k2, [yo, k7, yo, k2tog, k6] 12 times, k1. 195 sts.

Row 99: Using B, k. 195 sts.

Rows 100–103: Using D, k. 195 sts. PM at both ends of row 102.

Row 104: (Inc row) Using A, k1, [yo, [k2, yo, k2tog] 4 times] 12 times, k2. 207 sts.

Row 105: Using A, k. 207 sts.

Rows 106–107: Using B, k. 207 sts.

Rows 108–109: Using B, [k10, yo, k2tog] 17 times, k3. 207 sts.

Row 110: (Inc row) Using D, k1, [k8, yo, k7, k2tog, yo] 12 times, k2. 219 sts.

Row 111: Using D, k. 219 sts.

Row 112: Using A, k1, [k1, winding yarn around tip of RHN twice] 217 times, k1. 219 sts.

Row 113: Using A, k1, [k1 drop extra lp from LHN] 217 times, k1. 219 sts.

Row 114: Using D, k2, [yo, k2tog] 108 times, k1. 219 sts.

Row 115: Using D, k.

Row 116: (Inc row) Using B, k2, [yo, k9, yo, k2tog, k7] 12 times, k1. 231 sts.

Row 117: Using B, k. 231 sts.

Row 118: Using D, k2, [yo, k2tog] 114 times, k1. 231 sts.

Row 119: Using D, k. 231 sts.

Row 120: Using A, k1, [k1, winding yarn around tip of RHN twice] 229 times, k1. 231 sts.

Row 121: Using A, k1, [k1 drop extra lp from LHN] 229 times, k1. 231 sts.

Row 122: (Inc row) Using E, k2, [yo, k19] 11 times, yo, k17, yo, k2tog, k1. 243 sts.

Row 123: Using E, k. 243 sts.

Rows 124–125: Using C, k. 243 sts.

Rows 126–127: Using two strands of D, k. 243 sts.

Row 128: (Inc row) Using two strands of D, k1, [(k3, k2tog, yo) 3 times, k5, yo] 12 times, k2. 255 sts.

Row 129: Using 2 strands of D, k. 255 sts.

Row 130: Using B, k2, [yo, k2tog] 126 times, k1. 255 sts.

Row 131: Using B, k. 255 sts.

Rows 132–133: Using A, k. 255 sts.

Row 134: (Inc row) Using C, k2, [(yo, k2tog) 10 times, yo, k1] 12 times, k1.

Row 135: Using C, k. 267 sts.

Row 136: Using B, k1, [k1 winding yarn around tip of RHN twice] 265 times, k1. 267 sts.

Row 137: Using B, k1, [k1 drop extra lp from LHN] 265 times, k1. 267 sts.

Rows 138–139: Using A, k. 267 sts.

Row 140: (Inc row) Using D, k1, [k11, yo, k9, k2tog, yo] 12 times, k2. 279 sts.

Row 141: Using D, k. 279 sts.

Row 142: Using C, k2, [yo, k2tog] 138 times, k1. 279 sts.

Row 143: Using C, k. 279 sts.

Rows 144–145: Using D, k. 279 sts.

Row 146: (Inc row) Using 2 strands of D, k1, [[k1 winding yarn around tip of RHN twice] 23 times, yo twice] 12 times, k1 winding yarn around tip of RHN twice, k1. 291 sts. PM at both ends of row.

Row 147: Using 2 strands of D, k1 [k1 dropping extra lp from LHN] 289 times, k1. 291 sts.

Rows 148–149: Using A, k. 291 sts. Using a 7 mm (size 10½) needle, cast off loosely knitwise.

Threading

Using a tapestry needle with a blunt point, thread into the spaces and not through the yarn. Use enough of the yarn to thread across the complete row without joins or puckering.

Row 64: With RS facing you, thread 1 or 2 strands of F through each st.

Row 102: With WS of shawl facing you, thread one strand of C immediately above the garter stitch ridge and one strand of C below the garter st ridge.

Row 146: With RS of shawl facing, thread one or two strands of A through each st.

Crochet Edging

To make bobble: work 1dtr into next sp, but do not pull through last 2 lps (2 lps on hook), work 2 foll dtr into same sp in same way (4 lps on hook), yo and pull through all 4 lps.

Using F and 6 mm (J-10) crochet hook, work a row of dc evenly across cast-off edge, making sure that there is a multiple of 6 sts + 6.

Row 1: 3ch (counts as dtr), miss next 2 sts, work 1 bobble into next st, 6 ch, 1 bobble into same st as last bobble, * miss 5 sts, work 1 bobble into next st, 6ch, 1 bobble into same st as last bobble, rep from * to last 3 sts, miss 2 sts, 1 tr in next st. Fasten off. Remove waste yarn. Pull the tail of A firmly to gather stitches and secure. With RS facing, using a 6 mm (size J-10) crochet hook and D used double, work a row of dc along the straight edge. Turn. 3 ch then work 1 ttr into each dc. Fasten off and weave in ends.

Tropical storm

The area between the lines of latitude that follow the equator around the middle of the Earth – the Tropic of Cancer in the Northern Hemisphere and the Tropic of Capricorn in the Southern Hemisphere – is known as the tropics. This area is the only part of the Earth where the sun arrives directly overhead at least once a year. It is hot, tropical and humid for the most part and includes rainforests and lush vegetation. Strange, almost alien creatures and plants flourish in these ecosystems, which boast brightly coloured plumage and foliage, and a dark, hot, humid and tempestuous environment.

Inspirations include vivid flowers, strange animals, exotic trees and plants, spiky green leaves, lush vegetation, layers of soil, and heat. Colours are vibrant and lush: bright greens, neon shades, velvety rich hues, deep reds, browns, violets and fuchsia.

Fibres and yarns come from plants in the environment, such as bamboo, banana and soy. Strong textures, sculptural knits and layers of fabric evoke the multiple layers of the tropical jungle.

1 Tropical birds have fantastic coloured plumage. **2** Bright primary colours play off each other. **3** Vivid pinks, purples and oranges clash regally. **4** Light under the canopy is scarce. **5** The tropics are home to weird and wonderful wildlife.

The rainforest

The dense canopies of very tall trees in the rainforest shut out the light and cast the ground below into semi-darkness, inhibiting growth on the forest floor. The canopy is home to monkeys, birds, tree frogs and snakes. The essential difference between a rainforest and a jungle is the thickness of this canopy. A jungle is a rainforest where the trees have thinned out, allowing sunlight to stream through and thus enabling vines, plants, trees and lush undergrowth to grow. It is difficult to walk through the tangled plant life.

There is an air of danger and mystery in these climes – strong emotions that can be harnessed in your knitting. The colours typically found among the flora and fauna serve only to highlight this ambience of strange, dramatic foreboding. When thinking of the plumage or petals of some of the species, bright, dazzling hues are what come to mind; energetic, almost unnaturally vivid hot pinks, electric blues, sultry blood reds and stunning violets all stand out against the backdrop of a luxuriant, fertile green.

6 Native fabrics echo colours from nature. 7 Indigenous crafts are worth looking for. 8 Vivid colours stand out against a green backdrop. 9 Tropical plants are as amazing as the birds. 10 Yarn textures are shiny and slinky, or matte and crisp. 11 Recycled sari silks make great yarn. 12 Basket-woven patterns are ripe for copying. 13 Hot reds are found where there ought to be greens.

9

10

11

12

13

Tropical colour Then there are the shapes: spiky carnivorous plants with teethlike protrusions, poisonous blobs of patterned skin to aid as camouflage or warn off predators, and the beautifully extravagant tail feathers and crown plumage of the mating ritual. All is not quite as it seems. Animals and plants frequently use beauty to attract their prey, and what seems simply alluring proves instead to be deadly.

All of these wonderful textures cry out to be captured in three-dimensional knits and lush, jewel-like, coloured, silky yarns. Bamboo grows in diverse climates but is often found in tropical regions. The fibre is smooth, with a sheen almost as iridescent as silk, which results in luminescent hues when dyed – perfect for translating the radiant shades of the rainforest. Fancy yarns with odd bobbles, fringes and spiky tendrils would also be a great choice. Knitting techniques can be used to great effect to create your own three-dimensional fabric. Bobbles and spikes can easily be made with clever use of shaping, and abstract shapes can be made separately from the fabric and applied afterwards. Stripes and chevrons of bright colours also evoke the diversity of animals, plants, shapes and colours and the menacing undertones of the rainforest.

14 Vibrant chevrons sing out against each other. **15** Spiky shapes are a direct inspiration from nature. **16** Multicolours don't have to be acid bright and are toned down here. **17** The colours from nature are always more exotic than the imagination can create.

Your Mood Board

Unless you are on a long trip, it is unlikely that you'll be visiting the jungle. However, you can look in *National Geographic* or, better still, visit your local botanical garden for inspiration.

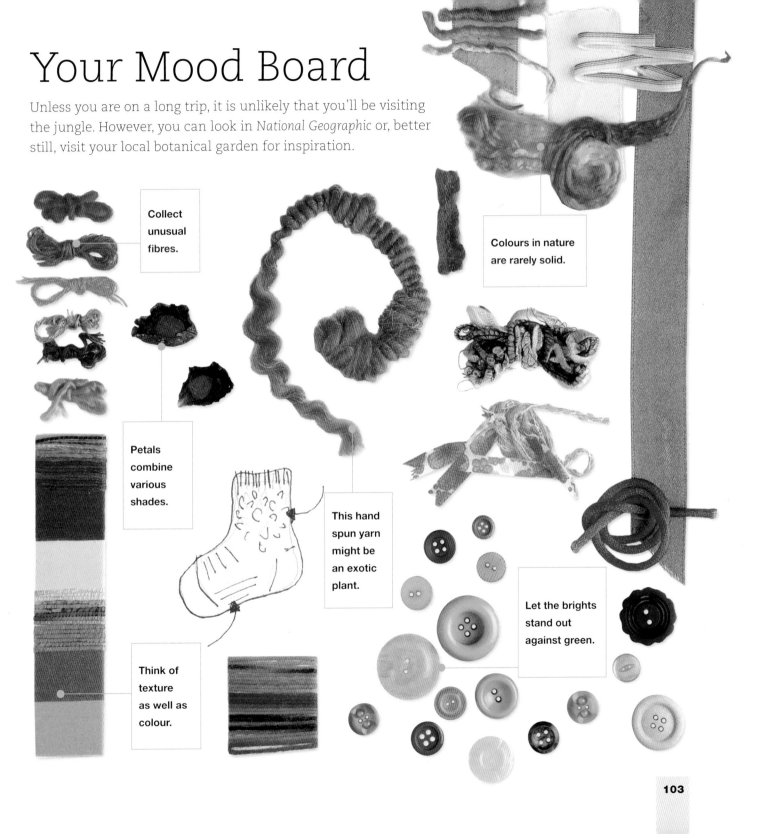

Collect unusual fibres.

Colours in nature are rarely solid.

Petals combine various shades.

This hand spun yarn might be an exotic plant.

Let the brights stand out against green.

Think of texture as well as colour.

Tree Frog Socks

These socks were inspired by the poisonous tree frogs that are indigenous to South America and apparently used to poison the darts of the local tribesmen. The frogs have brightly coloured reptilian skin to frighten away predators. The stitch in these socks features long threads stretched over the surface to suggest scales or darts.

Colinette Jitterbug yarn is 4-ply, which is perfect for socks, and comes in a glittering array of colourways, lending itself to a tropical theme. The colours change along the length of the yarn because it is space-dyed, so you don't have to keep changing yarns and it makes a unique pattern every time. This merino yarn is also easy-care and can be washed and dried in a machine, making it even more attractive to a knitter.

Materials

- 1 x Colinette Jitterbug sock yarn, 100% merino wool, 100 g (3½ oz), 297 m (323 yds.) in Fire
- 3 mm (size 2) and 3.25 mm (size 3) dpn
- Cable needle

Tension/Measurements

Small: shoe size adult 2–4 (34–37)

Medium: shoe size adult 5–7 (38–40)

You can easily adjust these sizes to fit your foot by following instructions under the foot section.

Yarn alternative: Any sock yarn that achieves the required tension. This yarn is roughly sportweight, somewhere between 4-ply and DK. If you wish to wear them regularly, make sure that the yarn you choose is sock yarn, which is usually easy-care, a mix with a man-made fibre in it, and tightly spun for durability.

These multicoloured yarns are partly space-dyed – the colour changes automatically as you knit – and some have multiple colours embedded in their structure so they do the work for you.

Kw2 – K1, wrapping yarn twice around the needle.

C3R – (cable 3 right): Slip next 2 sts onto cn, hold at back of work, k next st from left-hand needle, then k sts from cn.

C3L – Slip next st onto cn, hold at front of work, k next 2 sts from left-hand needle, k st from cn.

Leg

Using 3 mm (size 2) needles, CO 60(66) sts and join for working in the round, PM to mark beg of rnd. Work 12 rnds 1 x 1 rib (k1, p1). Change to 3.25 mm (size 3) needles and cont in pattern as follows:

Rnd 1: K2, (kw2) twice, *k4, (kw2) twice, rep from * to last 2 sts, k2.

Rnd 2: K2, sl2 (drop extra wraps), *k4, sl2 (drop extra wraps), rep from * to last 2 sts, k2.

Rnd 3: K2, sl2, *k4, sl2, rep from * to last 2 sts, k2. Rep last rnd twice more.

Rnd 6: *C3R, C3L, rep from * across rnd. Rep these 6 rnds 10 more times.

Divide for heel

Remove marker, knit across 30(30) sts, turn, leaving rem sts on needle, cont on these 30 sts as folls:

Row 1: Sl1, p to end.

Row 2: Sl1, k to end.

Rep these 2 rows, until 28(32) rows have been worked. Work row 1 once more.

Turn heel

Knit 17(17), Sl 1, k1, psso, k1, turn.
Sl 1, p5, p2tog, p1, turn.
Sl 1, k6, Sl 1, k1, psso, k1, turn.
Sl 1, p7, p2tog, p1, turn. Cont, working 1 more st each row until all heel sts have been worked. 18(18)sts.

Instep

Divide sts between needles, k across 18(18) heel sts, pick up and k 16(18)sts down edge of heel flap, PM, k 30(36) sts across top of foot, keeping to patt, PM2, pick up and k 16(18) sts up edge of heel flap. 80(90) sts.

Rnd 1: Knit to within 2 sts of 1st marker, k2tog, patt to 2nd marker, Sl 1, k1, psso, k to end of rnd.

Rnd 2: K to first marker, patt to 2nd marker, k to end.

Rep last 2 rnds until 60(64) sts rem.

Foot

Next rnd: K to first marker, work across 30(32) foot sts keeping to established 6 pattern rows, k to end. Next rnd: K to 1st marker, work across 30(36) foot sts keeping to established 6 patt rows, k to end.

Note: If you have longer or shorter feet, it is easy to adjust the pattern: just ignore the rnds stated here and continue working the foot until it reaches halfway up your big toe.

Toe

Rnd 1: K1, Sl 1, k1, psso, k to within 3 sts of 2nd marker, k2tog, k2, Sl 1, k1, psso, k to within 3 sts of 1st marker, k2tog, k1. 56(62) sts.

Rnd 2: Knit.

Rep last 2 rnds until 24(26) sts rem. Place 12(14) on each of 2 needles and knit together or graft together with Kitchener stitch.
Weave in ends.

Chevron Bag

The exotic nature of this theme deserves exciting and unusual yarns. Plants in a tropical ecosystem can provide many bizarre fibres, such as bamboo and banana. They both supply a shiny, luminescent yarn, that is perfect for conveying the vibrant colours of the rainforest and hot, hazy humidity of the tropics.

Bamboo yarn is a subtle, soft yarn reminiscent of silks, with a beautiful fluid drape. The colours it holds are deep and sultry. Banana provides a less-refined yarn but it is beautiful nonetheless with its intense sheen.

A chevron stitch is used for this project – the smooth yarn makes the chevrons look like razor-sharp menacing spikes. The colours and proportion make a stunning, eye-catching pattern, like the beauty of a tropical bird's plumage or the layered petals of a flowering vine.

Yarn alternative: There are plenty of bamboo, soy bean and seaweed yarns being produced at the moment. These cellulose-based, rather than protein-based, yarns have a silky quality that suits this project well.

Materials

- Be Sweet Bamboo, 100% bamboo, 50 g (1¾ oz), 110 m (120 yd) 1 of each:
  Yarn A: 618, palm green
  Yarn B: 659, hot pink
  Yarn C: 613, tangerine
  Yarn D: 609, peacock
  Yarn E: 673, blood red

- 1 x Frabjous Fibers 100% Banana Silk Yarn 200 g (7 oz), 145 m (159 yds.) in red

- 5.5 mm (size 9) needles

- 6.5 mm (size 10½) needles

- 2 rectangular wooden bag handles 12.7 x 7.6 cm (5 x 3 in)

- Lining fabric, 2 squares approx 27 x 27 cm (10½ x 10½ in)

- Two squares of shirt collar-stiffening fabric 27 x 27cm (10½ x 10½ in)

Measurements

Finished bag is roughly 27 cm (10½ in) wide and 32 cm (12½ in) long without handles

Tension

20 sts to 10 cm (4 in) over chevron pattern in bamboo yarn

cdk – central decrease knitwise. Insert right-hand needle into next 2 stitches as if to knit the two stitches together and slip these stitches onto right-hand needle. Knit next stitch on left-hand needle, then pass both slipped stitches together over the stitch just knitted.

m1k – make 1 stitch by picking up the bar between the needles and knitting into the back of it, inc – make 1 stitch by knitting into the front and back of next st.

Sides of bag

Using a pair of 5.5 mm (size 9) needles and Yarn A, cast on 60 sts.

Row 1: * K1, m1k, k8, cdk, k8, m1; rep from * to last st, replace k8, m1 for k7, inc into next st.
Row 2: Knit.
Rows 3–8: Repeat rows 1 and 2. Break Yarn A.
*Join Yarn B.

Row 9: * K1, m1k, k8, cdk, k8, m1; rep from * to last st, replace k8, m1 for k7, inc into next st.
Row 10: Purl.
Rows 9 to 10 form pattern. Cont in patt changing colours in stripes as follows:
Break Yarn B.
Join Yarn C and work two rows patt.
Break Yarn C.
Join Yarn D and work two rows patt.
Break Yarn D.
Join Yarn E and work two rows patt.
Break Yarn E, rep from *.
Join Yarn A, work 4 rows in patt, then following same sequence (B, C, D, E) work stripes of 4 rows of each.

Join Yarn A, work 6 rows in patt, then following same sequence (B, C, D, E) work stripes of 6 rows of each, ending with Yarn E. Break Yarn E.

Cont in Yarn A, knit 8 rows even, without shaping. Cast off all stitches.

Make one more bag side in this way.

Handles

Using 6.5 mm (size 10½) needles and banana yarn, cast on 10 sts and knit in st st for 15 cm (6 in). Cast off.

Fold over strip to make 7.5- cm (3- in) long rectangle. Sew along edges to fasten. Attach one short end to centre top edge of one side of bag. Fold strip once more in same direction and loop through bag handle. Attach remaining loose end firmly to centre of bag with other end. Make one more handle attachment in same way.

Finishing

Sew each wrong side of bag to a square of stiffening fabric, matching the flat top bag edges to tops of stiffening fabric. The fabric should stop just before the zigzag lower edge of the bag.

Sew up side seams of bag with mattress stitch, matching the stripes, and along the bottom of bag by sewing backstitch along the zigzag edge.

Place the two squares of lining fabric together and sew around three sides using running stitch on a sewing machine or by hand using backstitch. Attach to inside of bag, wrong-sides together, so that the seams of the lining cannot be seen.

Palm Scarf, Hat and Mittens Set

Knitting does not necessarily have to produce a flat fabric. With visual information as vibrant, unusual and edgy as tropical flora and fauna, a flat monochrome knit just won't do. By playing around with the chevron technique, a three-dimensional, exciting piece of knitting can be created. When the position of increases and decreases is varied at certain intervals, little peaks, or spikes, can be made. These can be pushed into the reverse of the fabric to produce convex and concave shapes, creating different textures, depending on how you arrange them. Here, all the horizontals with three 'spikes' are allowed to stand proud, while the ones with two 'spikes' are pushed into hollows. The fabric can gather naturally into spiky folds and creases or lie open, with the peaks and valleys on display. Add to this the natural gradation of bright colours in the yarn, and you end up with a fun, slightly crazy pattern.

By changing just a few elements, such as the amount of rows you knit before changing the position of the increasing and decreasing, or the way in which you feed in the colours of yarn, you can produce a totally different effect. The hat has just one repeat of the stitch pattern, which causes the fabric to respond in a different way, creating a more subtle puckered texture. The mittens are left in stocking stitch, for practicality, and also to allow the stunning colours of the yarn to really shine. Using this variegated yarn is a great way to introduce many colours into one piece without buying large amounts of yarn.

Materials
- Yarn A: 1 x Manos del Uruguay, kettle-dyed pure wool, 100% wool, 100 g (3½ oz) 126 m (138 yd) in green 2364
- Yarn B: 2 x Noro Kureyon, 100% wool, 50g (1¾ oz) 100 m (109 yd) in 154
- Yarn C: 1 x Noro Kureyon, 100% wool, 50g (1¾ oz) 100 m (109 yd) in 180
- 5.5 mm (size 9) needles
- 3.5 mm and 4 mm (sizes 3 and 6) needles
- 4 mm (G-6) crochet hook

Measurements
Scarf: Approx 160 cm (63 in) long and 15 cm (6 in) wide when not gathered in spikes

Hat: To fit head approx 48 cm (19 in)

Mittens: Approx 15 cm (6 in) length, to fit child aged 5–8 yrs

Tension
Approx 20 sts to 10 cm (4 in) over chevron st

Yarn alternatives: The Noro yarn is hand-dyed in Japan and stripes naturally in these exotic colours. Any Aran or worsted-weight yarn would do – solid or space-dyed.

Scarf

Cast on 12 sts, using 5.5 mm
(size 9) needles and Yarn A.

Row 1: Purl.
Row 2: Knit 1, inc in next st, k2, sl1,
k1, psso, k2tog, k2, inc in next st, k1.
Row 3: Purl.
Row 4: As row 2.
Row 5: Purl. Cast on 10 sts at end of
row (22sts).
Row 6: Knit 1, inc in next st, k2, sl1,
k1, psso, k2tog, k2, inc in next 2 sts,
k2, sl1, k1, psso, k2tog, k2, inc in next
st, k1.
Row 7: Purl.
Row 8: As row 6.
Row 9: Purl.
Row 10: As row 6. Cast on 10 sts at
end of row (32sts).
Row 11: Purl.
Row 12: Knit 1, inc in next st, k2, sl1,
k1, psso, k2tog, k2, *inc in next 2 sts,
k2, sl1, k1, psso, k2tog, k2, * rep from *
to last 2 sts, inc in next st, k1 (32sts).
Row 13: Purl.

Rep last two rows once more
then change to Yarn B.

Pattern for scarf continues as
follows:
Row 1: Knit 1, inc in next st, k2, sl1,
k1, psso, k2tog, k2, *inc in next 2 sts,
k2, sl1, k1, psso, k2tog, k2, * rep from *
to last 2 sts, inc in next st, k1.
Row 2: Purl.
Rep last two rows twice more.
Row 7: Knit 1, k2tog, k2, inc in next
2 sts, k2,* sl1, k1, psso, k2tog, k2, inc
into next 2 sts, k2, rep from * to last 3

sts, k2tog, k1.
Row 8: Purl.
Rows 9–12: Rep last 2
rows twice more.

These 12 rows form pattern. Rep
these rows until scarf measures
approx 150 cm (59 in) long (or
desired length) alternating between
the three yarns randomly to vary
the stripes. End with a row 1.

Next row: Cast off 10 sts, (1 st rem
on right needle after cast off) inc into
next st, k2, sl1, k1, psso, k2tog, k2, inc
in next 2 sts, k2, sl1, k1, psso, k2tog,
k2, inc in next st, k1. (22 sts).
Next row: Purl.
Next row: K1, inc into next st, k2, sl1,
k1, psso, k2tog, k2, inc in next 2 sts,
k2, sl1, k1, psso, k2tog, k2, inc in next
st, k1.
Next row: Purl.
Rep last 2 rows once more.
Next row: Cast off 10sts, (1 st rem on
right needle after cast off) inc into
next st, k2, sl1, k1, psso, k2tog, k2, inc
in next st, k1. (12 sts).
Next row: Purl.
Next row: K1, inc into next st, k2, sl1,
k1, psso, k2tog, k2, inc in next st, k1.
(12sts).
Next row: Purl.
Rep last 2 rows twice more.
Cast off all sts.

Finishing

Sew in all ends. When steaming,
make sure that you do not
press the spikes. Just allow the

heat and steam to relax them,
otherwise they may not be as
three-dimensional as you wish.

Hat

Using 5.5 mm (size 9) needles and |
Yarn A, cast on 74 sts.
Work 4 cm (1½ in) in 2 x 2 rib.
Cont in st st for 3 cm (1¼ in),
change to Yarn B or C (or a
mixture of both) and work pattern
repeat as for scarf as folls:

Row 1: Knit 2, inc in next st, k2, sl1,
k1, psso, k2tog, k2, *inc in next 2 sts,
k2, sl1, k1, psso, k2tog, k2, * rep from *
to last 3 sts, inc in next st, k2.
Row 2: Purl.
Rep last two rows twice more.
Row 7: Knit 2, k2tog, k2, inc in next
2 sts, k2,* sl1, k1, psso, k2tog, k2, inc
into next 2 sts, k2, rep from * to last 4
sts, k2tog, k2.
Row 8: Purl.
Rows 9–12: Rep last 2
rows twice more.

Change back to Yarn A and
work an additional 7 cm (2¾ in)
straight in st st. Cast off all sts.

Finishing

Fold strip in half widthwise, and
sew seam along cast-off sts and side
edge. Sew in all ends.
Optional: Make two tassels
or pompoms and attach
to top corners of hat.

Mittens

Using Yarn B or C (or a mixture) and 3.5 mm (size 3) needles, cast on 34 sts.
Work 6 rows in 1 x 1 rib. Change to 4 mm (size 6) needles.
Work 6 rows in st st.
Cont in st st; work increases as follows:
Row 1: K 16, inc in next 2 sts, k to end (36sts).
Row 2 and every alt row: Purl.
Row 3: Knit.
Row 5: K17, inc in next 2sts, k to end (38sts).
Row 7: Knit.
Row 9: K17, inc in next st, k2, inc in next st, k to end (40 sts).
Row 10: Purl.
Knit 2 more rows st st.

Divide for thumb as follows:

Next row: K25, turn, leaving rem 15 sts on holder.
Next row: P8, cast on 3 sts, turn (11sts). Work 8 rows st st on these 11 sts for thumb.
Next row: K1, (k2tog) 5 times.
Next row: Purl.
Break yarn and thread through rem 6 sts, pull up to gather and fasten securely.
With right-side facing, rejoin yarn to 17 sts before thumb, k17, knit 3 sts from cast-on sts at bottom of thumb, k to end of row (35 sts).
Work another 13 rows st st.

Shape top as follows:

Row 1: K3, k2tog, k5, k2tog, k11, k2tog, k5, k2tog, k3 (31sts).
Row 2 and every alt row: Purl.
Row 3: K3, k2tog, k4, k2tog, k9, k2tog, k4, k2tog, k3 (27 sts).
Row 5: K3, k2tog, k3, k2tog, k8, k2tog, k3, k2tog, k2 (23 sts).
Row 6: K3, k2tog, k2, k2tog, k7, k2tog, k2, k2tog, k1 (19 sts).
Row 7: K1, (k2tog) 9 times (10 sts).
Break yarn and thread through rem 10 sts, pull up to gather and fasten securely.
The mittens are both alike, so make one more mitten in the same way.

Finishing

Join side and thumb seams and weave in ends securely.

Using 4 mm (G-6) hook and whichever yarn you wish; work a length of chain approx 110 cm (43½ in) long, or desired length, and attach either end to the cuff of a mitten. Use chain to thread through the arms of the child's coat to prevent lost mittens.

Country pastels

Long, balmy summer days spent running through fields of corn or lying in long grass, sky gazing with birds and butterflies flitting above; farms and animals surrounding country houses and cottage industries – all of these idyllic images of the countryside have informed this theme. Rural traditional craft processes – spinning and knitting fleece straight from the sheep, basketry and hand weaving – are all part of the romantic pastoral idyll. The images all have a very romantic and dreamlike notion, perhaps fostered by images from films or 1960s hippy album covers. But there is nothing wrong with that.

The atmosphere is one of slowing time, the haze of the sun's heat on a field of golden rapeseed, the echoes of birdsong, and a feeling of calm contentedness among the golden sun-drenched colours. There are plenty of pretty floral colours to choose from: the many sunshine shades of yellow; sweet pastels of wildflowers, such as foxgloves, lilacs, cowslips and daisies. The slick of bright reds and purples in poppies and tulips, fluffy whites of seeds and pollen drifting on the wind, grass green and sky blue – all are capable of inspiring beautiful knits.

1 Country cottage idyll. **2** Pale, muted colours and soft textures. **3** Long, rustling grasses. **4** Fair Isle patterns in pastel colourways. **5** Handspun yarn from local breeds. **6** Sheep among the heathers.

7

8

9

10

11

12

13

Summery yarns

Many fibres would suit this theme, with cotton being an obvious choice for summer knitted items. The fibre derives from seed heads of the cotton plant. Straw can be knitted and experimented with, making a direct reference to haystacks and perhaps basket weaving. Raffia could be used as a more practical alternative; although made from palms, it closely resembles straw. These could be made into wicker bags or summer hats with wide brims to shade the sun.

Corn fibre is an unusual choice. The quality of this yarn is smooth, light and beautiful, with a drape not unlike some cottons, but with a gorgeous, subtle sheen and a velvety softness reminiscent of petals. Light-reflecting silks and shiny yarns are a great choice for imitating sun-dazzled hues. Soft, fluffy wool, straight from the sheep, can be spun and knitted into country-style blankets, pillows and household items.

7 Garden and meadow flowers and grasses. **8** Simple knit-and-purl patterns. **9** Intarsia on a quilt evokes country crafts and heritage. **10** Plain cables in muted tones. **11** Faded paintwork and natural woods and materials. **12** Natural silk yarns echo the faded paint and flowers. **13** Easy crochet stitches and pastel colours work well for cute kids' projects.

Construction

The techniques used in knitting can be very pretty and elaborate in this theme. Petals can be knitted into the fabric or made separately and attached onto garments. Whole-flower shapes and corsages can be knitted, with great potential for experimentation with fancy yarns and unusual stitches. Intarsia can be utilized to good effect, placing floral shapes into the knitting, or try using cross-stitch and embroidery to incorporate floral motifs.

There are techniques, such as corn sheaf and butterfly stitches, already known in knitting terms. You could play around with these or make up your own stitches to resemble flowers or corn. Traditional rural stitches that resemble country tweeds or Fair Isles, reworked in pretty floral colours, can be used to great effect to create a country casual look for walks through the fields.

14 Knitted flowers can be used to embellish your creations. **15** Inspiration from nature. **16** Several coloured yarns knitted together create a bright palette. **17** Meadow flowers.

Your Mood Board

Pretty floral prints and vintage lace, leaf motifs and flower shapes – all contribute to this meadow-flower palette. Colours are muted and pale, brought together by Nature herself to create a relaxing whole.

Embroidery and lace in combination with colour and motif.

Sections of old garments cut up for new.

Palest tones sit among brighter sparks.

Flower-like buttons.

A leaf motif inspired by nature.

A knitted flower with button.

Loom Patchwork Blanket

In the past, especially in rural towns, knitting and spinning were seen as productive alternatives to resting at the end of the day. A woman's work is never done, and after a day's chores, there are reports of women documenting how many inches of knitting they had completed. In colonial America, for example, as with samplers, knitting was used to teach Bible passages—mittens were produced with whole verses knitted in Fair Isle twining around the palms and thumbs. The blanket in this pattern is a knitted take on those early quilts lovingly repaired by the colonial women, also taking inspiration from the practice of colonial girls learning to read and write through embroidered samplers and knitting.

Colonial women started quilting bees, still a nostalgic symbol of country life, to form bonds and lend support when times were hard and family members were absent. It was quite common to have the names of family members who had passed away embroidered on the quilts, and this led to the term "comforter" coming to describe these blankets. Here, both intarsia and embroidery are used to create traditional embellishments. To develop a unique family heirloom, mix and match these flourishes and create your own personal comforter by using the charts to incorporate your own phrases or sayings.

Materials

- Pear Tree 8-ply, 100% merino wool, 1¾ oz. (50 g), 107 yd. (98 m)
  10 x Robin's Egg
  8 x Turkey
  6 x Blush
  8 x Grass
  2 x Blue Sky

- Size 8 (5 mm) needles

Measurements

Width of hexagons: approx 7 in. (19 cm)

Finished quilt approx 47 x 53 in. (120 x 135 cm)

Gauge

21 sts to 4 in. (10 cm)

Yarn alternatives: Any DK or light worsted-weight yarn

B1—(k1, p1, k1, p1, k1) all into next st, (5sts). Turn and starting with a knit row, work 4 rows st st. Sl 1, k2tog, psso, k2tog, turn, k2tog and continue across row.

Construction

Using size 8 (5 mm) needles, cast on 21 sts, then choose from a variety of the following patches and work one after the other without binding off, in a long strip in your own personal pattern. (A chart of our arrangement can be seen on the following page.) The strips are either 7 or 8 hexagons long; after the last hexagon, bind off all sts, and weave in all ends. Sew strips together as shown in chart and embroider letters and numbers into plain squares, using alphabet chart, either like our blanket or with your own phrases or names.

Bobble patch

Row 1: Using size 8 (5 mm) needles, k1 row.

Row 2: Inc into first st by knitting into front and back of st (kfb), k to last st, kfb (23 sts). Rep last 2 rows once more. (25 sts).

Next row: K4, p to last 4 sts, k4.

Next row: Kfb, k to last st, kfb. (27sts). Rep last 2 rows until you have 39 sts.

Next row: K4, p to last 4 sts, k4.

Next row: Kfb, k 18, B1, k to last st, kfb (41sts).

Next row: K4, p to last 4 sts, k4.

Next row: K18, B1, k3, B1, k to end.

Next row: K4, p to last 4 sts, k4.

Next row: K2tog, k18, B1, k to last 2 sts, k2tog. (39sts).

Next row: K4, p to last 4 sts, k4.K2tog, k to last 2 sts, k2tog. Rep last two rows until there are 23 sts.

Next row: K.

Next row: K2tog, k to last 2 sts, k2tog (21sts).

Change color and move onto another patch.

Plain patch

Using size 8 (5 mm) needles, knit 1 row.

Next row: Inc into first st by knitting into front and back of st (kfb), k to last st, kfb. (23sts). Rep last 2 rows once more. (25 sts).

Next row: K4, p to last 4 sts, k4.

Next row: Kfb, k to last st, kfb (27sts). Rep last 2 rows until you have 41 sts.

Next row: K4, p to last 4 sts, k4.

Next row: K.

Next row: K4, p to last 4 sts, k4.

Next row: K2tog, k to last 2 sts, k2tog (39sts).

Next row: K4, p to last 4 sts, k4.

Next row: K2tog, k to last 2 sts, k2tog. Rep last two rows until there are 23 sts.

Next row: K.

Next row: K2tog, k to last 2 sts, k2tog (21sts).

Change color and move onto another patch and cont with pattern.

Turkey intarsia patch

Using size 8 (5 mm) needles, k 1 row.

Next row: Inc into first st by knitting into front and back of st (kfb), k to last st, kfb. (23sts).

Rep last 2 rows once more. (25 sts).

Next row: K4, p to last 4 sts, k4.

Next row: Kfb, k to last st, kfb (27sts). Rep last 2 rows until you have 33 sts.

Next row: Cont in patt, but begin intarsia pattern as from first row of chart no 3. Rep last 2 rows until you have 41 sts.

Next row: Cont in intarsia pattern, k4, p to last 4 sts, k4.

Next row: K.

Next row: K4, p to last 4 sts, k4.

Next row: K2tog, k to last 2 sts, k2tog (39sts).

Next row: K4, p to last 4 sts, k4. (37 sts).

Next row: K2tog, k to last 2 sts, k2tog. Rep last two rows until there are 23 sts.

Next row: K.

Next row: K2tog, k to last 2 sts, k2tog (21sts).

People intarsia patch

Using size 8 (5 mm) needles, k 1 row.

Next row: Inc into first st by knitting into front and back of st (kfb), k to last st, kfb (23sts). Rep last 2 rows once more.

Next row: K4, p to last 4 sts, k4. (25 sts).

Next row: Kfb, k to last st, kfb. (27sts).

Next row: Begin intarsia pattern from row 1 of chart no 1 while continuing patt by rep last 2 rows until you have 41 sts.

Next row: Cont in intarsia pattern, k4, p to last 4 sts, k4.

Next row: K.

Next row: K4, p to last 4 sts, k4.

Next row: K2tog, k to last 2 sts, k2tog (39sts).

Next row: K4, p to last 4 sts, k4.
Next row: K2tog, k to last 2 sts, k2tog.
Rep last two rows until there are 23 sts.
Next row: K.
Next row: K2tog, k to last
2 sts, k2tog (21sts).

Follow the charts or create your own to make a personal statement or commemoration. Use the alphabet to spell out names or dates.
1. A couple holding hands.
2. The alphabet.
3. Traditional turkeys.

Color key

- ■ light blue
- □ white
- ▨ pink
- ■ red

Patch template

This template shows the arrangement of the colored segments on our "quilt." Follow this example, or make your own, arranging your patterned sections accordingly.

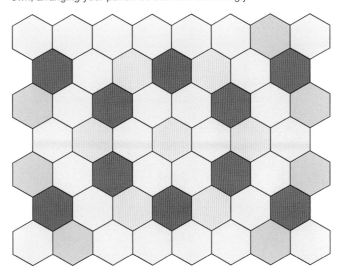

Chart 1

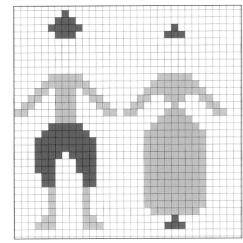

Chart 3

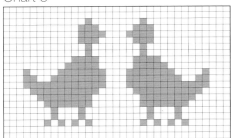

Chart 2

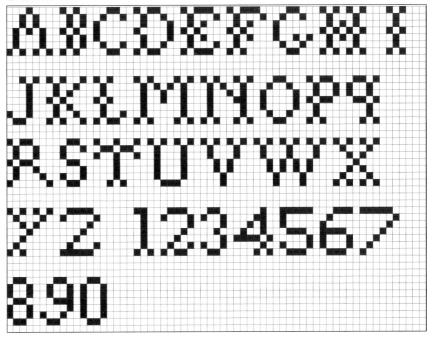

Iris Swing Top

In summer it is too warm to wear bulky wool knits, so silk is a perfect fiber, not only to create the soft, lightweight drape and a cooler fabric but also to add a bit of shine, which in a sunny climate shimmers beautifully. This pattern is inspired by the subtle sheen and stunning colors of flowers and petals, which the silk represents perfectly. The lacy petal stitch at the border reinforces this theme while being incredibly pretty and summery, and the cross-stitch floral panel at the bust combines a country-craft influence with a striking geometric pattern.

Yarn alternatives: Any sportweight or 4-ply yarn with shine and draping qualities would work well. Bamboo, viscose, or Lyocell yarns, for instance. Yarn quantities are based on average requirements and are therefore approximate.

Materials

- Yarn A: 7(8,8,9,9,10) x **Blue Sky alpaca and silk 50% alpaca, 50% silk, 1¾ oz. (50 g), 146 yd. (133 m) in 136, Champagne**
- Yarn B: 1(2,2,2,2,2) x **129 Amethyst**
- 1 each of: **123 Ruby, 130 Mandarin, 131 Kiwi, and 137 Sapphire**
- 1 yd. (1 m) x 1 in. (2.5 cm) wide grosgrain ribbon and sewing thread to match Yarn A
- Size 2 (3 mm) and 3 (3.25 mm) needles
- Size D-3 (3.25 mm) or E-4 (3.50 mm) crochet hook

Measurements

To fit bust

32	34	36	38	40	42	in.
81	86	91	97	102	107	cm

Actual bust size

32	34	36	38	40	42	in.
81	86	91	97	102	107	cm

Length to armhole
20 in. (51 cm)

Gauge

27 sts and 33½ rows to 4 in. (10 cm) square over st st on size 3 (3.25 mm) needles

Inc 1k—increase 1 stitch by knitting into the front and the back of the next stitch.

Inc 1p—increase 1 stitch by purling into the front and the back of the next stitch.

Figures in parentheses ( ) refer to larger sizes. Where only one set of figures is given, this applies to all sizes.

Back

Using size 3 (3.25 mm) needles and Yarn A, cast on 141(151:161:161:171:181) sts.
Row 1 * K1, p1; rep from * to last st, k1. Repeating 1st row forms moss stitch. Work 4 more rows moss st.

Begin leaf pattern

Row 1: K3, * k2tog, yo, k1, yo, sl1, k1, psso, k5; rep from * to last 8 sts, k2tog, yo, k1, yo, sl1, k1, psso, k3.
2nd and every alternate row: Purl.
Row 3: K2, * k2tog, [k1, yo] twice, k1, sl1, k1, psso, k3, rep from * to last 9 sts, k2tog, [k1, yo] twice, k1, sl1, k1, psso, k2.
Row 5: K1, * k2tog, k2, yo, k1, yo, k2, sl1, k1, psso, k1; rep from * to end.
Row 7: K2tog, * k3, yo, k1, yo, k3, sl 1, k2tog, psso; rep from * to last 9 sts, k3, yo, k1, yo, k3, sl1, k1, psso,.
Row 9: K1, * yo, sl1, k1, psso, k5, k2tog, yo, k1; rep from * to end.
Row 11: K1, * yo, k1, sl1, k1, psso, k3, k2tog, k1, yo, k1; rep from * to end.
Row 13: K1, * yo, k2, sl1, k1, psso, k1, k2tog, k2, yo, k1; rep from * to end.
Row 15: K1, * yo, k3, sl 1, k2tog, psso, k3, yo, k1; rep from * to end.
Row 17: K3, * k2tog, m1k, k1, m1k, sl1, k1, psso, k5; rep from * to last 8 sts, k2tog, m1k, k1, m1k, sl1, k1, psso, k3.
Row 19: K2, * k2tog, m1k, k3, m1k, sl1, k1, psso, k3, rep from * to last 9 sts, k2tog, m1k, k3, m1k, sl1, k1, psso, k2.
Row 21: K1, * k2tog, m1k, k5, m1k, sl1, k1, psso, k1; rep from * to end.
Row 23: K2tog, * m1k, k7, m1k, sl 1, k2tog, psso; rep from * to last 9 sts, m1k, k7, m1k, sl1, k1, psso.
Row 25: K1, * yo, k1, sl1, k1, psso, k5, k2tog, yo, k1; rep from * to end.
Row 27: K1, * yo, k1, sl1, k1, psso, k3, k2tog, k1, yo, k1; rep from * to end.
Row 29: K1, * yo, k2, sl1, k1, psso, k1, k2tog, k2, yo, k1; rep from * to end.
Row 31: K1, * yo, k3, sl 1, k2tog, psso, k3, yo, k1; rep from * to end.
Row 33: K3, * k2tog, m1k, k1, m1k, sl1, k1, psso, k5; rep from * to last 8 sts, k2tog, m1k, k1, m1k, sl1, k1, psso, k3.
Row 35: K2, * k2tog, m1k, k3, m1k, sl1, k1, psso, k3, rep from * to last 9 sts, k2tog, m1k, k3, m1k, sl1, k1, psso, k2.
Row 37: K1, * k2tog, m1k, k5, m1k, sl1, k1, psso, k1; rep from * to end.
Row 39: K2tog, * m1k, k7, m1k, sl 1, k2tog, psso; rep from * to last 9 sts, m1k, k7, m1k, sl1, k1, psso.
Row 40: Purl.
Cont in st st.

Shape for waist

Row 3: (RS) K2, k2tog, k48(52:56:55:58:62), k2tog, k33(35:37:39:43:45), ssk, k48(52:56:55:58:62), ssk, k2. 137(147:157:157:167:177) sts.

Beg with a purl row, work 3 rows st st.
Row 7: (RS) K2, k2tog, k46(50:54:53:56:60), k2tog, k33(35:37:39:43:45), ssk, k46(50:54:53:56:60), ssk, k2. 133(143:153:153:163:173) sts.
Beg with a purl row, work 3 rows st st.
Row 11: (RS) K2, k2tog, 44(48:52:51:54:58), k2tog, k33(35:37:39:43:45), ssk, k44(48:52:51:54:58), ssk, k2. 129(139:149:149:159:169) sts.
Beg with a purl row, work 3 rows st st.
Row 15: (RS) K2, k2tog, k42(46:50:49:52:56), k2tog, k33(35:37:39:43:45), ssk, k42(46:50:49:52:56), ssk, k2. 125(135:145:145:155:165) sts.
Beg with a purl row, work 3 rows st st.
Row 19: (RS) K2, k2tog, k40(44:48:47:50:54), k2tog, k33(35:37:39:43:45), ssk, k40(44:48:47:50:54), ssk, k2. 121(131:141:141:151:161) sts.
Beg with a purl row, work 3 rows st st.
Row 23: (RS) K2, k2tog, K38(42:46:45:48:52), k2tog, k33(35:37:39:43:45), ssk, k38(42:46:45:48:52), ssk, k2. 117(127:137:137:147:157) sts.
Beg with a purl row, work 3 rows st st.
Row 27: (RS) K2, k2tog, k36(40:44:43:46:50), k2tog, k33(35:37:39:43:45), ssk, k36(40:44:43:46:50), ssk, k2. 113(123:133:133:143:153) sts.
Beg with a purl row, work 3 rows st st.
Row 31: (RS) K2, k2tog, k34(38:42:41:44:48), k2tog, k33(35:37:39:43:45), ssk, k34(38:42:41:44:48), ssk, k2.

109(119:129:129:139:149) sts.
Beg with a purl row, work 3 rows st st.

Row 35: (RS) K2, k2tog, k32(36:40:39:42:46), k2tog, k33(35:37:39:43:45), ssk, k 32(36:40:39:42:46), ssk, k2. 105(115:125:125:135:145) sts.
Beg with a purl row, work 3 rows st st.

Row 39: (RS) K2, k2tog, k30(34:38:37:40:44), k2tog, k33(35:37:39:43:45), ssk, k30(34:38:37:40:44), ssk, k2. 101(111:121:121:131:141) sts.
Beg with a purl row, work 3 rows st st.

Row 43: (RS) K2, k2tog, k28(32:36:35:38:42), k2tog, k33(35:37:39:43:45), ssk, k28(32:36:35:38:42), ssk, k2. 97(107:117:117:127:137) sts.
Beg with a purl row, work 3 rows st st.

Row 47: (RS) K2, k2tog 0(1:1:0:1:1) time, k30(32:34:37:38:40), k2tog 0(0:1:0:0:1) time, k33(35:37:39:43:45), ssk 0(0:1:0:0:1) time, k30(32:34:37:38:40), ssk 0(1:1:0:1:1) time, k2. 97(105:113:117:125:133) sts.
Beg with a purl row, work 3 rows st st.

Row 51: (RS) K2, k2tog 0(0:1:0:0:1) time, k93(101:105:113:121:1 25), ssk 0(0:1:0:0:1) time, k2. 97(105:111:117:125:131) sts.
Beg with a purl row, work 3 rows st st.

Shape bodice

Row 1: (RS) K2, m1k, knit to last 3 sts, m1k, k2. 99(107:113:119:127:133) sts.
Beg with a purl row, work 5 rows st st.
Rep last 6 rows twice and 1st row once more. 105(113:119:125:133:139) sts. ******
Cont in st st without shaping until back measures 17½ in. (44 cm) from

cast-on edge, ending with a purl (WS) row.
Change to size 2 (3 mm) needles.
Next Row: (RS) * K1, p1; rep from * to last st, k1.
Next Row: * P1, k1; rep from * to last st, p1.
Repeating these 2 rows forms 1x1 rib.
Cont in rib until back measures 20 in. (51 cm), ending with a WS row.
Bind off in rib.

Front

Work as for back to ******.
105(113:119:125:133:139) sts. Cont in st st without shaping until front measures 14½ in. (37 cm) from cast-on edge, ending with a purl (WS) row.

Shape yoke

Row 1: (RS) K36(39:41:43:45:47), m1k, k33(35:37:39:43:45), m1k, k36(39:41:43:45:47). 107(115:121:127:135:141) sts.
Row 2: P37(40:42:44:46:48), m1p, p33(35:37:39:43:45), m1p, p37(40:42:44:46:48). 109(117:123:129:137:143) sts.
Row 3: K38(41:43:45:47:49), m1k, k33(35:37:39:43:45), m1k, k38(41:43:45:47:49) . 111(119:125:131:139:145) sts.
Row 4: Purl.
Rows 5–46: Cont in st st, placing a marker along row 5 to mark first row of embroidered pattern.
Front should measure 20 in. (51 cm) from cast-on edge. This band is where you will place the embroidery.

Shape armholes

Cont in st st.
Bind off 6(6:8:8:8:10) sts at beg of next 2 rows. 99(107:109:115:123:125) sts.
Next Row: (RS) K2, k2tog, knit to last 4 sts, ssk, k2. 97(105:107:113:121:123) sts.
Next Row: P2, sl1, p1, psso, purl to last 4 sts, p2tog, p2. 95(103:107:111:119:121) sts.
Rep last 2 rows 0(1:1:1:2:2) times and the first of these 2 rows 0(0:0:1:0:0) time more. 95(99:101:105:111:113) sts.
Purl 0(0:0:1:0:0) row. Bind off.

Shoulder straps (make 2)

Using size 3 (3.25 mm) needles and Yarn A, cast on 13 sts.
Work in moss stitch as given for the back until strap measures 15¼ (15½, 16, 16½, 17, 17½) in. [39 (40, 41, 42, 43, 44) cm]
Bind off in moss st.
PM on both side edges ⅜ in. (2 cm) from cast-on edge and PM on both side edges ⅜ in. (2 cm) from bound-off edge. PM at center of cast-on and bound-off edges. Break off Yarn A.

Sash and Ribbon

Using Yarn B and size 3 (3.25 mm) needles, cast on 13sts and work in moss st as for straps until sash measures the same length as the circumference under the bust.

Bow

Using size 3 (3.25 mm) needles and Yarn A, cast on 37 sts.

Row 1: K1, * P1, K1; rep from * to end.
Repeating row 1 forms seed/moss stitch.
Cont in moss stitch until bow measures 26½ (27, 28, 28¾, 29½, 30½) in. [67 (69, 71, 73, 75, 77) cm.]
Bind off in moss stitch.

Bow center

Using size 3 (3.25 mm) needles and Yarn B, cast on 13 sts.
Work in moss stitch as for the bow until strip measures 5½ in. (14 cm).
Bind off in moss stitch.

Embroidered band

Following the embroidery chart on page 131, stitch the pattern in cross stitch, along the front band, using each square to represent one cross. The marker denotes the first row and the pattern reaches to side seams of front.

Finishing

Block each piece, avoiding the rib.
Join side seams, matching bound-off edge of back with front armhole bound-off edges.
Using a size D-3 (3.25 mm) or E-4 (3.5 mm) crochet hook and Yarn B, with RS facing and starting at right underarm seam, work a row of single crochet across back bound-off edge to left underarm.
Turn, work 1 chain, and then work a second row of single crochet across the front only.
Fasten off and weave in ends.

Straps

PM at 2¼ (2¼, 2¼, 2¾, 2¾, 3¼) in. [6 (6, 6, 7, 7, 8) cm] from side each edge of bound off edges of back and front.

Cut two lengths of grosgrain ribbon to match the shoulder strap length. Center the ribbon on the WS of the straps and stitch ribbon into place with matching sewing thread.

Attach straps to dress, the side markers of the straps matching the bound-off edges of the back and the front, and the markers at the center of the cast-on and bound-off edges of the straps, matching the markers on the bound-off edges of the back and front.

Attach sash by sewing directly underneath the floral band all around with ends meeting at center back.

Join the cast-on and bound-off edges of the bow strip. With the seam just sewn at center back, work through both layers of the bow on both sides of the seam to hold the bow shape in place.
With RS of bow facing, place the bow center around the middle of the bow. Fold the cast-on and bound-off edges to the WS of the bow and sew into place over the center back sash join.

Stitch the bound-off ends of the ties into place on WS of the bow. Sew the bow into place on the back of the top.

Embroidery chart

Follow the chart below using cross stitch.

Color key

- Kiwi
- Sapphire
- Amethyst
- Ruby
- Mandarin

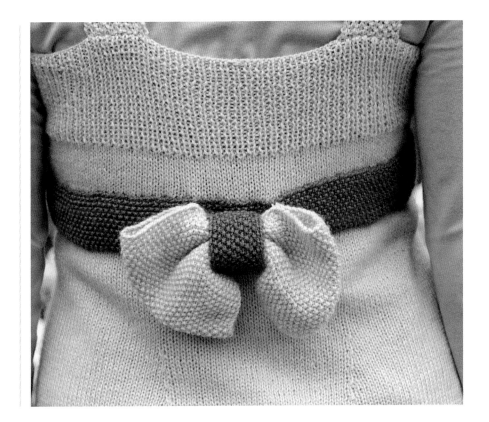

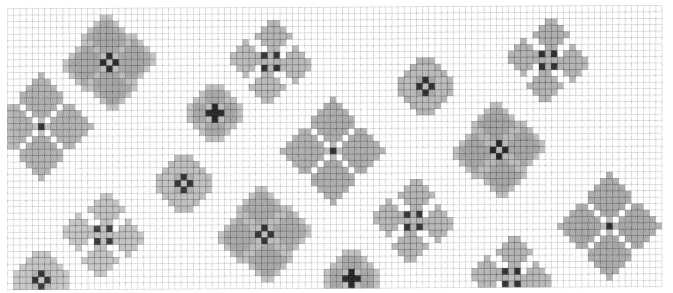

Materials

- **Debbie Bliss Pure Silk, 100% silk, 2 oz. (50 g) 137 yd. (125 m) per ball, 1 each: light green 005, lilac 009, pink 012, pale blue 014, lime 015, lemon 016, and red 019**

- **Small amount of smooth waste yarn in a contrast color**

- **Size 6 (4 mm) needles**

- **Tapestry needle**

Measurements

Length
47¼ in. (120 cm)

Width
4 in. (10 cm)

Each square
4 x 4 in. (10 x 10 cm)

Gauge

Each square measures 4 x 4 in. (10 x 10 cm) square over garter stitch and over leaf pattern on size 6 (4 mm) needles.

Exact gauge is not a requirement.

Note: Yarn quantities are based on average requirements and are therefore approximate.

Yarn alternatives: Any double knit or worsted-weight yarn or yarns that produce an elegant drape.

Summer Silk Scarf

A quintessential summer look can be effortlessly achieved by throwing on an elegantly simple silk scarf. This colorful scarf can be worn in many ways, even around the waist as a belt, to add a dash of color and life to a summer wardrobe. The luxury of the silk provides the scarf with a heavy, sumptuous drape and the colors of the yarn add a velvety iridescent sheen.

The three-dimensional petal shapes evoke the floral theme, and the textured patches can be added at more random intervals or more frequently as desired. Due to its construction, the scarf can be made longer or shorter, simply by adding more or fewer squares. Have fun with this pattern and enjoy the process—the squares are made using shaping in such a way that, at first, one cannot see what the end result will be.

Square with leaf

(Make 3 in different colors)
Using size 6 (4 mm) needles and waste yarn, cast on 4 sts.

1st and 2nd rows: Knit. Break waste yarn. Join Yarn A.

Row 1: (WS) Leaving a long tail at the beginning of the row, knit. Thread the tail at the beginning of the row through a tapestry needle and thread through all 4 sts on the knitting needle, leaving sts on the needle. Remove tapestry needle, and continue working from the ball.

Row 2: (RS) * (K1, yo, k1) all into next st; rep from * 3 times. 12 sts.

Row 3: * K1, p1, k1; rep from * 3 times. 12 sts.

Row 4: * (K1, yo) twice, k1, m1k; rep from * twice, (k1, yo) twice, kfb. 24 sts.

Row 5: * K2, p3, k1, m1k; rep from * twice, k2, p3, kfb. 28 sts.

Row 6: * K2, (k1, yo) twice, k3, m1k; rep from * twice, k2, (k1, yo) twice, k2, kfb. 40 sts.

Row 7: * K3, p5, k2, m1k; rep from * twice, k3, p5, k1, kfb. 44 sts.

Row 8: * K5, yo, k1, yo, k5, m1k; rep from * twice, k5, yo, k1, yo, k4, kfb. 56 sts.

Row 9: * K4, p7, k3, m1k; rep from * twice, k4, p7, k2, kfb. 60 sts.

Row 10: * K7, yo, k1, yo, k7, m1k; rep from * twice, k7, yo, k1, yo, k6, kfb. 72 sts.

Row 11: * K5, p9, k4, m1k; rep from * twice, k5, p9, k3, kfb. 76 sts.

Row 12: * K9, yo, k1, yo, k9, m1k; rep from * twice, k9, yo, k1, yo, k8, kfb. 88 sts.

Row 13: * K6, p11, k5, m1k; rep from * twice, k6, p11, k4, kfb. 92 sts.

Row 14: * K6, ssk, k7, k2tog, k6, m1k; rep from * twice, k6, ssk, k7, k2tog, k5, kfb.

Row 15: * K7, p9, k6, m1k; rep from * twice, k7, p9, k5, kfb. 92 sts.

Row 16: * K7, ssk, k5, k2tog, k7, m1k; rep from * twice, k7, ssk, k5, k2tog, k6, kfb.

Row 17: * K8, p7, k7, m1k; rep from * twice, k8, p7, k6, kfb. 92 sts.

Row 18: * K8, ssk, k3, k2tog, k8, m1k; rep from * twice, k8, ssk, k3, k2tog, k7, kfb. .

Row 19: * K9, p5, k8, m1k; rep from * twice, k9, p5, k7, kfb. 92 sts.

Row 20: * K9, ssk, k1, k2tog, k9, m1k; rep from * twice, k9, ssk, k1, k2tog, k8, kfb.

Row 21: * K10, p3, k9, m1k; rep from * twice, k10, p3, k8, kfb. 92 sts.

Row 22: * K10, sl 1K, k2tog, psso, k10, m1k; rep from * twice, k10, sl 1K, k2tog, psso, k9, kfb. 88 sts.

Row 23: * K22, m1k; rep from * twice, k21, kfb. 92 sts.

Row 24: * K23, m1k; rep from * twice, k22, kfb. 96 sts.

Row 25: * K24, m1k; rep from * twice, k23, kfb. 100 sts.

Bind off (on RS).

Square without leaf

(Make 8 in random colors)
Using size 6 (4 mm) needles and waste yarn, cast on 4 sts. 1st and 2nd rows Knit. Break waste yarn and join Yarn A.

Row 1: (WS) Leaving a long tail at the beginning of the row, knit. Thread the tail at the beginning of the row through a tapestry needle and thread through all 4 sts on the knitting needle. Remove tapestry needle and continue working from the ball.

Row 2: (RS) * (K1, yo, k1) all into next st; rep from * 3 times. 12 sts.

Row 3: Knit. 12 sts.

Row 4: * K3, m1k; rep from * twice, k2, kfb. 16 sts.

Row 5: * K4, m1k; rep from * twice, k3, kfb. 20 sts.

Row 6: * K5, m1k; rep from * twice, k4, kfb. 24 sts.

Row 7: * K6, m1k; rep from * twice, k5, kfb. 28 sts.

Row 8: * K7, m1k; rep from * twice, k6, kfb. 32 sts.

Row 9: * K8, m1k; rep from * twice, k7, kfb. 36 sts.

Row 10: * K9, m1k; rep from * twice, k8, kfb. 40 sts.

Row 11: * K10, m1k; rep from * twice, k9, kfb. 44 sts.

Row 12: * K11, m1k; rep from * twice, k10, kfb. 48 sts.

Row 13: * K12, m1k; rep from * twice, k11, kfb. 52 sts.

Row 14: * K13, m1k; rep from * twice, k12, kfb. 56 sts.

Row 15: * K14, m1k; rep from * twice, k13, kfb. 60 sts.

Row 16: * K15, m1k; rep from * twice, k14, kfb. 64 sts.

Row 17: * K16, m1k; rep from * twice, k15, kfb. 68 sts.

Row 18: * K17, m1k; rep from * twice, k16, kfb. 72 sts.

Row 19: * K18, m1k; rep from * twice, k17, kfb. 76 sts.

Row 20: * K19, m1k; rep from * twice,

k18, kfb. 80 sts.
Row 21: * K20, m1k; rep from * twice, k19, kfb. 84 sts.
Row 22: * K21, m1k; rep from * twice, k20, kfb. 88 sts.
Row 23: * K22, m1k; rep from * twice, k21, kfb. 92 sts.
Row 24: * K23, m1k; rep from * twice, k22, kfb. 96 sts.
Row 25: * K24, m1k; rep from * twice, k23, kfb. 100 sts.
Bind off (on RS).

Triangle with leaf

(Make 2 in random colors)
Using size 6 (4 mm) needles and Yarn A, cast on 1 st.
Row 1: (RS) (K1, yo, k1) all into next st. 3 sts.
Row 2: K1, p1, k1. 3 sts.
Row 3: (K1, yo) twice, kfb. 6 sts.
Row 4: K2, p3, kfb. 7 sts.
Row 5: K2, (k1, yo) twice, k2, kfb. 10 sts.
Row 6: K3, p5, k1, kfb. 11 sts.
Row 7: K5, yo, k1, yo, k4, kfb. 14 sts.
Row 8: K4, p7, k2, kfb. 15 sts.
Row 9: K7, yo, k1, yo, k6, kfb. 18 sts.
Row 10: K5, p9, k3, kfb. 19 sts.
Row 11: K9, yo, k1, yo, k8, kfb. 22 sts.
Row 12: K6, p11, k4, kfb. 23 sts.
Row 13: K6, ssk, k7, k2tog, k5, kfb. 22 sts.
Row 14: K7, p9, k5, kfb. 23 sts.
Row 15: K7, ssk, k5, k2tog, k6, kfb. 22 sts.
Row 16: K8, p7, k6, kfb. 23 sts.
Row 17: K8, ssk, k3, k2tog, k7, kfb. 22 sts.
Row 18: K9, p5, k7, kfb. 23 sts.
Row 19: K9, ssk, k1, k2tog, k8, kfb. 22 sts.
Row 20: K10, p3, k8, kfb. 23 sts.
Row 21: K10, sl 1K, k2tog, psso, k9, kfb. 22 sts.

Row 22: K21, kfb. 23 sts.
Row 23: K22, kfb. 24 sts.
Row 24: K23, kfb. 25 sts.
Bind off (on RS).

Sewing the squares

Remove the waste yarn and pull the tail of Yarn A to gather the stitches. Thread the Yarn A tail through a tapestry needle.
Put the two diagonal edges together to make a square. With the right-side, facing and working from the center of the square to the bound-off edge, insert the tapestry needle from bottom to top (not from back to front, or front to back) through the st at the end of the first garter ridge on the right-hand edge, then insert the tapestry needle from bottom to top through the end st of the first garter ridge on the left-hand edge. * Insert the tapestry needle from bottom to top through the st at the end of the next garter ridge on the right-hand edge, then insert the tapestry needle from bottom to top through the end st of the next garter ridge on the left-hand edge. Repeat from * until the seam is completed, pulling the sewing thread gently to close the seam.

Finishing

Block each square and the two triangles by damp finishing. Pin out each piece to shape, then spray with water, or steam, making the corners of the squares and the points of the triangles sharp, while not flattening the garter stitch ridges or the leaves.

Join four plain squares into a strip using mattress stitch, inserting the sewing needle between the bound off edge and the garter ridge below it, not pulling the sewing thread too tightly, so that the seam mimics a garter stitch row between the garter ridges. Make another group of four squares. Place the squares with a petal in the center and at either end of the scarf, making a long strip. Join the bound-off edge of one triangle with leaf to one end of the strip and the bound-off edge of the second triangle to the other end of the strip. Weave in all ends.

6

Desert sands

When thinking of desert scenery,

images that come to mind are of dry, dusty terrain with little vegetation, resulting in a color palette of dusky reds, earthy browns, and warm tones. In Africa the Masai tribe wears red as a link to the Earth, to show their love for it. This theme celebrates the sun, high temperatures, and dry, hot desert terrain.

The heat of the sun's rays should be taken into account, with warm tones like reds, oranges, browns, and golden yellows in abundance. In hot countries brightly colored houses and garments work especially well, with the warm light lending a glistening iridescence to them. White is also a typical color used for houses and clothing, to better reflect light and heat. Putting white next to bright colors also highlights the beauty and intensity of these colors. These factors should be considered in the color choices and design of fabrics in this theme.

1 An oasis in the sand. **2** Sandy tans and metallic shimmer. **3** Metallic chevron.
4 Space-dyed and flecked yarn introduces color. **5** Luxury softness of chenille.
6 Windswept sand dunes.

In the exotic countries with this intense parched heat, subtle hues of red, indigo, and gold are woven in rugs, brilliant saris, and ikat woven garments. A sensory overload of color emanates from ornaments, accessories, and swaths of silk, available to buy in bazaars and intricate, refined floral prints and embroidery. Theatrical, sparkling ornamentation on hems and hangings abound. Sometimes a wealth of information can be a hindrance, so it is advisable to concentrate on one area. A lovely contrast here is matte versus shiny, and silk versus wool, which is a representation of the dryness and matte sand as opposed to the shimmering of heat clouds above it, the camel hide in comparison to the silky garments and embellishment of nomad travelers.

Contrasting textures

The luminosity of the colors in the polished shine of silk yarn and fabric, as opposed to rich, matte wools, is a beauty to behold. This luster can also be replicated with viscose yarns or silk mixes. Even with the intense heat, knitting is practiced throughout these hot countries. Many Mongols in the Gobi desert raise sheep and goats, using fiber from their flock to make felt to create hats, socks, and tents, which are warm and water-resistant, especially for the cool nights. These felts form a great contrast to the shiny silks and can be used together to create textural interest.

7 Rich colors and shimmering jewels from the souk. **8** A landscape sculpted by the harsh wind and sun. **9** Ripples and dunes emulated in a knitted fabric. **10** Dark, dry red earth. **11** Shadows and stripes. **12** A range of natural reds and blues to choose from. **13** Ethnic and tribal arts of nomadic tribes. **14** Silhouettes of giant cacti against a red sky.

10

11

12

13

14

The wool and silk could even be used together to knit a piece that is then felted.

Uzbek and other central Asian nomads used braids, tassels, and woven trims to embellish their tents, garments, and the harnesses of the animals used to carry their loads. Woolen ends or horsehair were braided or wrapped and decorated with tassels, shells, beads, and metal disks, almost like sequins, all of which would make perfect ornamentation for knitted fabrics.

Animal hides. A great way to bring in pattern and color is with animal skins. From the bold monochrome stripes of the zebra to the uneven blotches of a giraffe, these skins can be easily transformed into knitted intarsia patterns, while a golden lion's mane may inspire textural fringing ideas or the use of a fur yarn or stitch.

This theme is exciting and colorful, with many different avenues and facets to explore in a joyous and almost irreverent way. Enjoy the beauty of the fabrics, but most important, be sure to choose colors that shimmer and sparkle as if lit by intense sunshine, to evoke a feeling of diversity and beauty.

15 Faux animal skins. **16** Bright colors faded by the sun and sand. **17** Camels decorated with handmade tassels and beaded fringing.

Your Mood Board

Sand colors, along with the rich reds and oranges of the rock and sky, combine beautifully with turquoises and neutrals. Beads and metallics add a glimpse of glamor.

Color bands of equal width for striped patterns.

Simple sketches for ideas.

Braids and ribbon.

Snippets of frayed silk fabrics.

Natural and polished wooden buttons.

Dust Socks

The pattern chosen for the top of these ankle-length socks represents the ripples of windblown sand over desert dunes. This easy stitch makes the pattern less regimented and more random, like nature. Just change the regularity of the purl ridges. It is also easy to change the length of the socks by adding more rows of the pattern, remembering that if you want to make knee-length or longer socks, you will need to shape the socks by increasing and decreasing. Socks are great to experiment with because you can easily use one simple sock pattern and change the color and/or stitch structure with little change to the pattern.

Materials

- 2 x Lorna's Laces Shepherd sock yarn, solid natural color, 80% superwash wool, 20% nylon, 2¼ oz. (60 g), 215 yd. (196 m)

- Size 1 (2.25 mm) dpn

Gauge/Measurements

To fit small adult shoe size 4–6 (34–36)

You can adjust these sizes for your length of foot by following instructions under foot section.

Alternative yarns: Any sock yarn that will achieve the required gauge. This yarn is roughly sock-weight; a sportweight or 4ply. Make sure that the yarn is sock yarn if you wish to wear them regularly. Look for easy-care, a mix including a man-made fiber that is very tightly spun for durability.

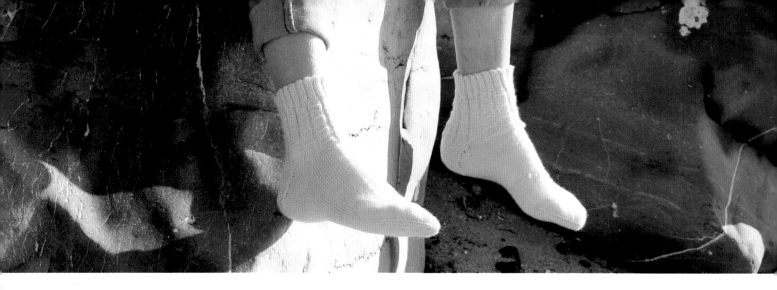

Special abbreviations

Kw2—K1, wrapping yarn twice around the needle.

C3R—(cable 3 right). Slip next 2 sts onto cable needle, hold at back of work, k next st from left-hand needle, then k sts from cable needle.

C3L—Slip next st onto cable needle, hold at front of work, k next 2 sts from left-hand needle, k st from cable needle.

Leg

Using size 1 (2.25 mm) needles, cast on 70 and join for working in the round. Place marker for beg of rnd. Knit 2 x 2 rib for 1¼ in. (3 cm).

Bamboo pattern

Rnd 1: (and every alt row) (K5, p2) 10 times.
Rnd 2: (K5, p9) to end.
Rnd 4: (K5, p2) to end.
Rnd 6: P7, (k5, p9) to last 7 sts, k5, p2.
Rnd 8: (K5, p2) to end.
Rep these 8 rnds to form bamboo patt.
Work in patt for 40 rows. (70 sts).

Reinforce heel flap

Work on next 35 sts for heel as folls:
Row 1: *K1, s1, rep from * to last st, K1. (35, 38 sts). Turn.
Row 2: Purl.
Repeat these two rows until 26(32) rows have been worked altogether.

Turn heel

Row 27: K24, k2tog, k1, turn.
Row 28: P15, p2tog, p1, turn.
Row 29: K16, k2tog, k1, turn.
Row 30: P17, p2tog, p1, turn.
Cont in this way, working one more st each row until all sts have been worked. (25 sts).
Knit 25 sts.
Pick up and knit 16 sts down side of heel flap, PM.

Knit across 35 sts of instep, pm.
Pick up and knit 16 sts up other side of heel flap (92 sts).
Rejoin for working in the rnd.

Shape gusset

Rnd 1: K to within 3 sts of m, k2tog, k to 2nd m, sl1, k1, psso, k to end of rnd. 90 sts.
Rnd 2: Knit.
Repeat these last 2 rows until there are 70 sts.

Foot

Cont in st st without decreasing for 2¾ in. [7 cm], or until foot measures to halfway up big toe for a longer sock, ending at first marker.

Toe

Rnd 1: K1, sl1, k1, psso, k to within 3 sts of 2nd m, k2tog, k2, sl1, k1, psso, k to within 3 sts of 1st m, k2tog, k1. (66 sts).
Rnd 2: Knit.
Repeat these 2 rounds until 16 sts remain, with 8 sts on each needle. Knit together or graft the rem stitches together with Kitchener stitch.

Kashmir Scarf

There is an ancient tradition all over Asia, and among nomadic communities in general, of decoration by braiding and knotting to create tassels. Braids were originally used on the long ends of a woven warp to tidy it and to strengthen the woven fabric, so it would not fray, but gradually they moved to other fabrics; even tassels braided from hair were used as ornamentation. Fringes from nomads' tent decorations and traveling bags are the inspiration for this scarf. Extravagant tassels are an interesting way to finish knitted garments, especially scarves and wraps, adding movement, length, and a tidy, refined edge.

Traditional braids would be brightly colored and highly decorative; hence, the inclusion of the recycled sari silk in the embellished edge of the scarf. Intense color added into the neutral base yarn is a beautifully understated textural contrast that adds an iridescent quality, integrating the opulent colors of the hot climes yet guaranteeing the scarf's versatility.

Llama yarn is utilized as the base fabric. The soft, matte, hairy quality is a great contrast to the shiny silk fibers of the sari yarn. The sample swatches on page 148 demonstrate how another rare fiber can be used. The cashmere is a refined, lighter fiber, that can be used for added luxury. The colors chosen highlight how foreground tones can be affected by the surrounding colors.

Materials

- Yarn A: 3 x 3½ oz. (100 g) balls of Adriafil Llama Classic yarn, 50% llama, 50% wool, approx 131 yd. (120 m) in shade 063
- Yarn B: 1 x 3½ oz. (100 g) ball of Recycled Sari Silk yarn
- Sizes 10¾ and 11 (7 mm and 8 mm) needles

Measurements

Scarf measures 9½ in. (24 cm) wide and 59 in. (150 cm) long

Gauge

15 sts and 18 rows to 4 in. (10 cm) over stockinette stitch

Yarn alternatives: Use any weight yarn you wish; simply change the amount of sts to cast on, relative to your new gauge, remembering to keep it an odd number to make the moss st pattern work. If you plan to use the same weight, use a heavy worsted or chunky-weight yarn, with a variegated yarn in the same weight for the sari silk contrast. This yarn, being recycled from old saris by cooperatives in Nepal, varies in color from ball to ball and even meter to meter. Choose the skein with the colors you wish to use, and wind the balls so that different colors occur at certain points in your design.

Directions

Using size 10¾ (7 mm) needles, cast on 37 sts and work in moss (seed) st patt as follows:

K1, *p1, k1, rep from * to end of row. Rep this row to form patt.
Work 1 in. (2.5 cm) moss st and cont as follows.
Row 1: (RS) K1, p1, k1, p1, k1, k to last 5 sts, work these 5 sts in moss st, following patt.
Row 2: (WS) K1, p1, k1, p1, k1, p to last 5 sts, work these 5 sts in moss st, following patt.
Rep these 2 rows until work measures 5 in. (13 cm) from cast-on edge, ending with a wrong side row (row 2).

Change to size 11 (8 mm) needles and cont as follows, working rows 1 and 2 in Yarn A and 3 and 4 in Yarn B.
**Row 1: K1, *sl 1 purlwise wyif, k1, rep from * to end of row.
Row 2: K1, *yfwd, sl 1 purlwise, yb, k1, rep from * to end of row.
Row 3: K2, *sl 1 purlwise wyif, k1, rep from * to last st, k1.
Row 4: K2, *yfwd, sl 1 purlwise, yb, k1, rep from * to last st, k1.

These 4 rows form pattern. Cont in this patt, change colors as folls:
Rows 5–8: Yarn A.
Rows 9–10: Yarn B.
Rows 11–14: Yarn A.
Rows 15–16: Yarn B.
Rows 17–20: Yarn A.
Rows 21–22: Yarn B.
Rows 23–24: Yarn A**.

Change back to 10¾ (7 mm) needles and resume work as before:
Row 1: K1, p1, k1, p1, k1, k to last 5 sts, work these 5 sts in moss st, foll patt.
Row 2: K1, p1, k1, p1, k1, p to last 5 sts, work these 5 sts in moss st, following patt.
Cont in this way until work measures 51 in. (130 cm) from cast-on edge.

Change to size 11 (8 mm) needles and work 24 rows from ** to ** as before. Change back to size 10¾ (7 mm) needles and resume work as follows:
Row 1: K1, p1, k1, p1, k1, k to last 5 sts, work these 5 sts in moss st, following patt.
Row 2: K1, p1, k1, p1, k1, p to last 5 sts, work these 5 sts in moss st, following patt.
When work measures 58 in. (147.5 cm) work 1 in. (2.5 cm) of moss st patt as folls:
K1, *p1, k1, rep from * to end of row. Rep this row for 1 in. (2.5 cm).
Bind off all sts and sew in ends.

Finishing

Lightly block the wrap and add tassels as follows:
To make one tassel, cut 3 lengths of Yarn A, 20 in. (50 cm) long. Fold these lengths in half. With RS of work facing, pass a crochet hook up through the fabric along the edge of one short end, close to the cast-on or bound-off edges, but a few sts in. Draw the looped end of the strands through the fabric, pass the ends of the tassel through the loop and pull up to fasten. Make 5 tassels for each short end of the scarf, placing them approx 2 in. (5 cm) apart.
Pin the end of the fabric to a pillow and take half the strand from the first tassel, and half from the one next to it and make a double knot, or square knot. Use a pin to draw the knot into place. Work one more row of knots in the same way, to create diagonal knots, forming diamond shapes in the tassels. Trim the yarn into a neat edge of a standard length.

Alternative color swatches show the same pattern on different backgrounds. Instead of the Llama yarn, Debbie Bliss Pure Cashmere in black and ecru have been used. The effect of the sari silk is different in each one, either standing out or receding and blending in.

Cleo Evening Bag

There is a real beauty to an expanse of hot sand exposed to the intense rays of the sun, with its sparkling grains glittering in the light and the shimmering haze of heat above it. This is the inspiration for the elegant glitz of this evening bag. Here is an excuse—if you need one—for using fancy yarns encrusted with sequins, beads, or crystals, which catch the light beautifully, saving you the hassle of threading the yarn with beads beforehand or embellishing the bag after knitting. A yarn with a metallic thread is used, too, for a more subtle sheen. All of these decorations will ensure that the bag shines and sparkles under the evening stars, candlelight, or glow of the moon.

The scalloped stitch structure is reminiscent of sand dunes and ripples caused by the wind. It is a fairly simple stitch, which is very decorative and pretty. The color palette draws from the shades of the desert at night and the Bedouins' black tents on the distant horizon.

Alternative yarn: If using a single yarn, choose a chunky or heavy worsted yarn with sparkles, beads, or sequins, or experiment with plying many yarns together.

Materials

- Yarn A: One strand of chunky alpaca held together with one strand of Shingle and 2 strands of Kidsilk Night (you will need to spin off the ball of Kidsilk into 2 balls)

- 2 x Frog Tree chunky 100% alpaca, 2 oz. (50 g) 54 yd. (49 m) in 100 black

- 1 x Rowan Kidsilk Night, 67% superkid mohair, 18% silk, 10% polyester, 5% nylon, 1 oz. (25 g) 227 yd. (208 m) in 610 Starry Night

- 2 x Louisa Harding Shingle, 97% nylon, 3% polyester, 2 oz. (50 g) 87½ yd. 80 m in 05

- Yarn B: 1 x Tilli Tomas Asteroid, 100% spun silk with European glass beads, 3½ oz. (100 g) 80 yd. (73 m) in 297 burnt orange

- Size 10½ (6.5 mm) needles

- Cable needle

- Purse frame, approx 8½ in. (22 cm) wide

- Fabric to line bag, approx 16 in. x 11 in. (41 cm x 28 cm)

Measurements

Bag approx 8 in. (20 cm) deep by 11 in. (28 cm) wide

Gauge

Approx 16 sts to 4 in. (10 cm) over pattern

last 2 sts, p2.
Rep last 2 rows once more.
Row 9: K1, C2R, k1, C2L, *k5, C2R, k1, C2L, rep from * to last st, k1.

Cont in A, work 3 rows st st, beg with p row.
Row 13: Change to B, knit.
Row 14: K7, *p3, k7, rep from * to end of row.
Row 15: Change to A, k7, *sl3, k7, rep from * to end.
Row 16: P7, *sl3, p7, rep from * to end of row.
Rep last 2 rows once more.

Row 19: K6, *C2R, k1, C2L, k5, rep from * to last st, k1.
Row 20: Cont in A, purl.
Now work rows 1 to 9 once more, work 1 row purl in A, then work rows 13 to 20. Work rows 3 to 9 once more, then change to B and work 4 rows garter st. Bind off all sts.
Make one more bag side in the same way.

Finishing

Sew up cast-on edges and side seams of back and front. Fold the lining fabric in half lengthwise and sew to match the shape of the bag. Attach the lining to the bag by sewing along garter st top. Attach bag to the purse frame, all along the bound-off edge. Depending on the frame, you will either need to secure with an all-purpose adhesive glue and/or sew the bag and the purse frame together.

Special abbreviations
C2R—cable 2 right. Place next st on cable needle, and hold at back of work, k next st, then k st from cable needle.

C2L—cable 2 right. Place next st on cable needle and hold at front of work, k next st, then k st from cable needle.

Bag side (make 2)

Using the four strands of yarn held together that make up Yarn A, cast on 47sts.
Row 1: Knit.
Row 2: Purl.
Row 3: Change to Yarn B and knit.
Row 4: K2, p3, *k7, p3, rep from * to last 2 sts, k2.
Row 5: Change to Yarn A, k2, sl3, *k7, sl3, rep from * to last 2 sts, k2.
Row 6: P2, sl3, *p7, sl3, rep from * to

Yarn Directory

From silks to bamboos, from alpacas to mohairs

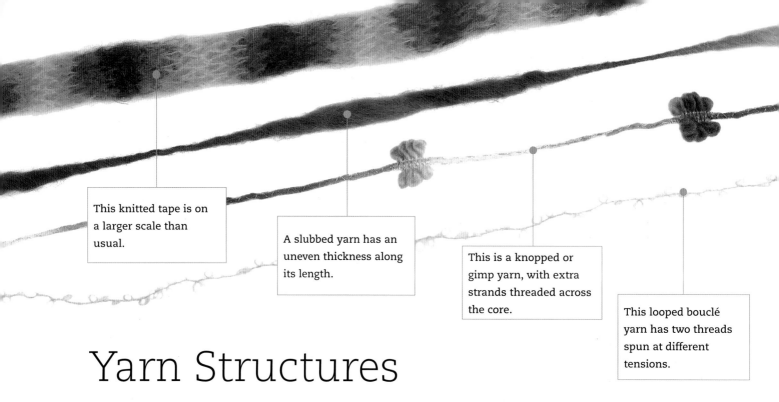

This knitted tape is on a larger scale than usual.

A slubbed yarn has an uneven thickness along its length.

This is a knopped or gimp yarn, with extra strands threaded across the core.

This looped bouclé yarn has two threads spun at different tensions.

Yarn Structures

To understand more about how a yarn is constructed, you must know about the fibers mainly used in this process.

Staples and filaments

First, there are *staple fibers*, which are of a limited, usually very short length. These can be as small as ³⁄₈ in. (1 cm). In order to form a yarn with these fibers, they have to be spun or twisted together into longer lengths. The spinning process can form many different textures. Examples of these types of fibers are wool and cotton.

The other type of fibers are called *filaments*, which are longer fibers that can be measured in yards or meters or, if man-made, even in miles. Examples of a natural filament include silk fibers, which gain smoothness from this filament length.

Single yarn The simplest strand of fiber—a single yarn—is a mass of fibers bonded into one yarn by spinning or twisting. A yarn can be spun or plied in many ways to create smooth or textured yarns.

Woolen This is not necessarily a yarn made from wool fibers, but of course, wool can be used. It is just the term used to describe short staple fibers of varying lengths that are spun to produce an airy, fluffy, warm yarn that is elastic.

Worsted A worsted yarn is formed from longer staple fibers, similar in length, that have been combed to ensure that the staples are parallel, creating an extra-smooth yarn when spun. The resulting yarn is strong and inelastic. It is extremely useful to know the difference between these two types of yarn when deciding on the fiber to use for a garment, because the woolen spun will be naturally warmer for cold winter days, and the worsted yarn will produce a cooler garment for warm summer evenings.

Roving Roving is an unspun mass of fibers, drawn or rubbed into a single strand, so that they are parallel to each other. This is usually the state of carded fibers: the stage prior to spinning worsted yarns. This is not necessarily a yarn, but it can be knitted as one, providing a super-bulky effect.

Plied yarn A plied yarn is made by twisting together two or more single yarns in one direction. This direction can either be to the left, which is called s (counterclockwise), or the right, which is called z (clockwise) twists. Plying yarns makes them stronger and more regimented.

Blended yarn This yarn comprises more than one type of fiber.

Double and twist yarn This two-color yarn is spun by twisting together yarns of different colors to form a spiral effect.

Marl or mottled This is a process in which two singles of differing solid colors, or dyed with differing techniques, are doubled and spun into a single yarn.

Novelty or fancy yarns Yarns that have irregularities placed into them during the spinning process.

Slub A slub is produced by adding the yarn to be spun at differing speeds so that the resulting yarn varies in thickness. A slub can also be added to the yarn being spun by inserting "bumps" of fiber from a separate source.

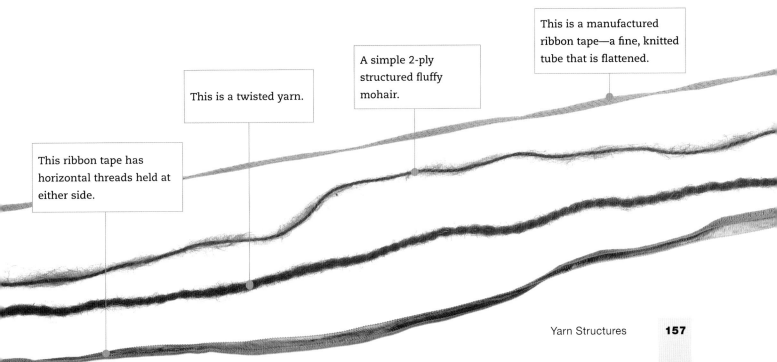

This is a manufactured ribbon tape—a fine, knitted tube that is flattened.

A simple 2-ply structured fluffy mohair.

This is a twisted yarn.

This ribbon tape has horizontal threads held at either side.

Yarn Types

Loops

When two or more threads are spun together, the tension each yarn is held at can contribute to the ultimate texture of the yarn. A looped yarn consists of two singles held at different tensions when spun so that the looser yarn buckles up and twists into clearly defined circular loops at regular intervals along the final yarn.

Within this group are bouclé yarns, which are formed in the same way but have smaller full-circle or semicircular loops positioned at irregular intervals along the length of yarn. A gimp yarn is created by binding an irregular single with a regular single at differing tensions to create graduating, semicircular loops and bumps along the yarn.

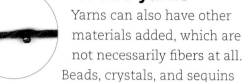

Coils, worms, or beehives

A coiled yarn is also called a worm or beehive, due to its texture of satisfyingly fat, coiled segments. The yarn is formed in a similar way to the loops, by holding two singles at differing tensions and allowing one to wrap tightly around the tense central core.

Knots, or knopps, can be made in a similar way, with one single held tense and the remaining thread or threads delivered in greater quantities at certain intervals, making a coiled bunch, or knot, of fiber.

Beaded yarns

Yarns can also have other materials added, which are not necessarily fibers at all. Beads, crystals, and sequins can be threaded onto a central core at intervals and spun within the fiber to create a single thread, out of which beads protrude. This type can also be made as a plied yarn, by plying the beaded thread together with one or more other singles.

Other ornamentation, such as small ribbons and other small snippets of fabric, can also be added to yarns when spun, by trapping them between two single plies. However, these can produce unstable yarns, with the added extras prone to falling off the final fabric.

A yarn made in a similar way to this is fur yarn, which is created by trapping many loose, long hairlike strands between the two binding single plies. It unsurprisingly knits up to resemble an animal's fur. Eyelash yarn tends to be a sparser version of fur, with long hairlike strands. It is usually bound together with very fine plies, making it thin and flimsy to work with, often easier to knit alongside another yarn to add texture and to define the stitches. Be careful if using these unstable yarns for baby clothing or toys, because the threads can come off in a baby's mouth.

Tapes and ribbons

A ribbon yarn is a woven fabric strip, which is an extra-long and often more pliable version of what you usually expect a ribbon to be. A tape is a single-ply narrow fabric as well, and knits to good effect. A tape can also be a tube of knitting. Non-spun yarns are a fantastic opportunity for experimentation. It is easy and fun to create your own yarns from ribbons and fabric and other remnants you may find lying around in your stash. Cut up fabric into strips and knit with it, or alternatively, there are ready-cut recycled fabric "yarns" on the market. Other tips are to use a sewing machine to sew together little scraps of fabric and yarn or ribbon to create your own chenille-like yarn.

Non spun yarns

Chenille is a velvety yarn with a luxurious pile created from a woven fabric with many runs, cut to form loose ends. Chenille often sheds from these loose ends.

Some yarns are difficult to categorize. This flat "paper" yarn is made from linen with a viscose coating.

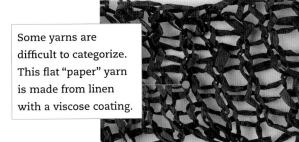

Yarn Weights

The thickness of yarn is called the weight. The classification of the exact thicknesses will vary from country to country and yarn to yarn but can be roughly arranged in groups like these:

Laceweight/2- or 3-ply

The gauge of the extra-fine yarns, often mohair for lace knitting, varies greatly.

Super fine/fingering weight/sock/4-ply

Often described as baby weight and used most commonly in children's clothing, Fair Isle, and sock knitting, this fine-weight yarn knits up to approximately 27–32 sts to 4 in. (10 cm).

Fine/sportweight/baby

Also used in baby clothes, this in-between weight knits to 23–26 sts to 4 in. (10 cm).

8-ply/double knitting/light

Double knitting, or DK, is a versatile, common thickness of yarn, with many uses. DK knits to roughly 21–24 sts per 4 in. (10 cm).

Medium/Aran/worsted weight/12-ply

A weight often used traditionally for cables and "Aran" knitting. Gauge is roughly 16–20 sts to 4 in. (10 cm).

Bulky/chunky weight

A much thicker yarn, used mainly for winter clothing, with a gauge of about 12–15 sts to 4 in. (10 cm).

Super bulky

The thickest of weights, knitted on very large needles, giving a gauge of 6–11 sts to 4 in. (10 cm).

Super fine

4-ply/fingering weight/sock/baby Often described as baby weight, used most commonly in children's clothing, and often used in Fair Isle and sock knitting. This fine weight knits up to approximately 27–32 sts to 10 cm (4 in).

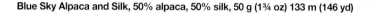

Blue Sky Alpaca and Silk, 50% alpaca, 50% silk, 50 g (1¾ oz) 133 m (146 yd)

Ggh Safari, 78% linen, 22% nylon, 50 g (1¾ oz) 140 m (153 yd)

Colinette Jitterbug sock yarn, 100% merino wool, 100 g (3½ oz) 297 m (324 yd)

House Of Hemp Expressions, 100% hemp, 4-ply, 50 g (1¾ oz) 84 m (92 yd)

Garnstudio Karisma, 100% pure new wool, 50 g (1¾ oz) 110 m (120 yd)

Jamieson's Shetland Spindrift, 100% pure shetland wool, approx. 25 g (1 oz) 105 m (115 yd)

Vuorelman Satakieli, 100% wool 4-ply, 100 g (3½ oz) 330 m (360 yd)

Koigu KPPPM hand-painted sock yarn, 100% merino wool, 50 g (1¾ oz) 160 m (175 yd)

Fleece Artist Sea Wool, 70% merino wool, 30% Seacell®, 112 g (4 oz) 350 m (383 yd)

Frabjous Fibers nettle yarn, 100% nettle, 90 g (3 oz) 183 m (200 yd)

Fine

Double knitting/8-ply/light Double knitting, or DK, is a versatile, common thickness of yarn, with many uses. DK knits to roughly 21–24 sts per 10 cm (4 in).

Kolláge yarns Cornucopia, 100% corn, 34 g (1 oz) 91 m (100 yd)

Noro Shikisai, 35% cotton, 22% acrylic, 15% silk, 15% kid mohair, 13% wool, 50 g (1¾ oz) 155 m (169½ yd)

Alchemy Silken Straw, 100% silk, 40 g (1½ oz) 216 m (236 yd)

Noro Ganpi Abaka Surabu, 40% Ganpi Abaka, 58% rayon, 2% nylon, 50 g (1¾ oz) 235 m (257 yd)

Ggh Linova, 74% cotton, 26% linen, 50 g (1¾ oz) 100 m (109 yd)

British Breeds Yarns Blue-Faced Leicester Double Knitting, 50 g (1¾ oz) 120 m (131 yd)

Be Sweet, 100% Bamboo, 50 g (1¾ oz) 120 m (131 yd)

Patons Orient, 50% polyamide, 30% acrylic, 15% mohair, 5% wool, 50 g (1¾ oz) 150 m (164 yd)

Alchemy Silk Purse, 100% silk, 50 g (1¾ oz) 149 m (163 yd)

Pear Tree 8-ply, 100% merino wool, 50 g (1¾ oz) approx. 98 m (107 yd)

Debbie Bliss Cotton dk, 100% cotton, 50 g (1¾ oz) 80 m (87 yd)

Debbie Bliss Pure Silk, 100% silk, 50 g (1¾ oz) 125 m (137 yd)

Hawthorne Heritage Crafts handspun semi-worsted Whitefaced Woodland yarn, naturally dyed 100 g (3½ oz) approx 255 m (279 yd)

Medium

Medium/Aran/worsted weight/10-ply A weight often used traditionally for cables and Aran knitting. Tension is roughly 16–20 sts to 10 cm (4 in).

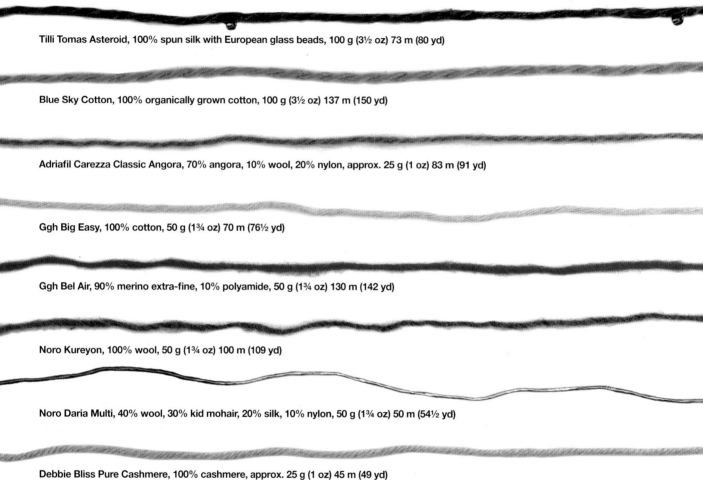

Tilli Tomas Asteroid, 100% spun silk with European glass beads, 100 g (3½ oz) 73 m (80 yd)

Blue Sky Cotton, 100% organically grown cotton, 100 g (3½ oz) 137 m (150 yd)

Adriafil Carezza Classic Angora, 70% angora, 10% wool, 20% nylon, approx. 25 g (1 oz) 83 m (91 yd)

Ggh Big Easy, 100% cotton, 50 g (1¾ oz) 70 m (76½ yd)

Ggh Bel Air, 90% merino extra-fine, 10% polyamide, 50 g (1¾ oz) 130 m (142 yd)

Noro Kureyon, 100% wool, 50 g (1¾ oz) 100 m (109 yd)

Noro Daria Multi, 40% wool, 30% kid mohair, 20% silk, 10% nylon, 50 g (1¾ oz) 50 m (54½ yd)

Debbie Bliss Pure Cashmere, 100% cashmere, approx. 25 g (1 oz) 45 m (49 yd)

Louisa Harding Grace, 50% silk, 50% wool, 50 g (1¾ oz) 110 m (120 yd)

Hawthorne Heritage Crafts, 100% Teeswater wool undyed and handspun, 100 g (3½ oz) 155 m (169 yd)

Medium heavy

Medium heavy/heavy Aran/worsted weight/Afghan/12-ply A slightly heavier weight than the traditional Aran.

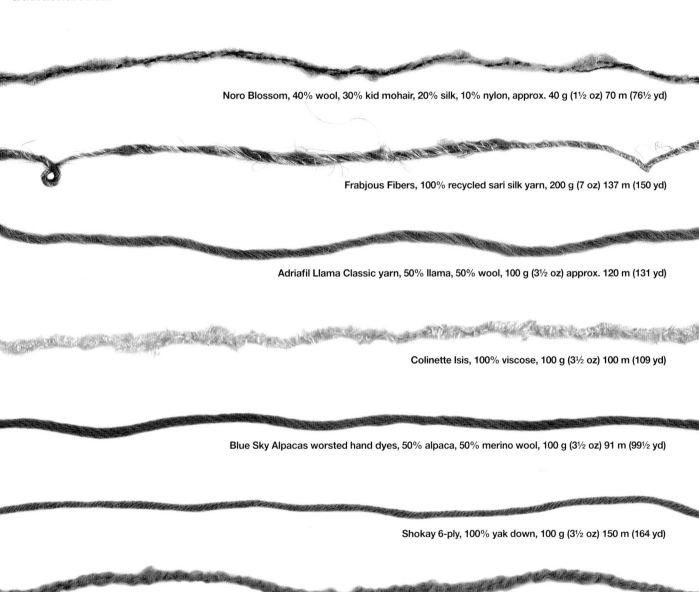

Noro Blossom, 40% wool, 30% kid mohair, 20% silk, 10% nylon, approx. 40 g (1½ oz) 70 m (76½ yd)

Frabjous Fibers, 100% recycled sari silk yarn, 200 g (7 oz) 137 m (150 yd)

Adriafil Llama Classic yarn, 50% llama, 50% wool, 100 g (3½ oz) approx. 120 m (131 yd)

Colinette Isis, 100% viscose, 100 g (3½ oz) 100 m (109 yd)

Blue Sky Alpacas worsted hand dyes, 50% alpaca, 50% merino wool, 100 g (3½ oz) 91 m (99½ yd)

Shokay 6-ply, 100% yak down, 100 g (3½ oz) 150 m (164 yd)

RY Classic Alpaca Soft, 65% cotton, 35% alpaca, 50 g (1¾ oz) 55 m (60 yd)

Novelty

Bouclé/slub/fancy/gimp/feathered This category encompasses all the other novelty and decorative yarns that don't fit in elsewhere. Special spinning techniques and different structures make this the most widely varying in weight and tension.

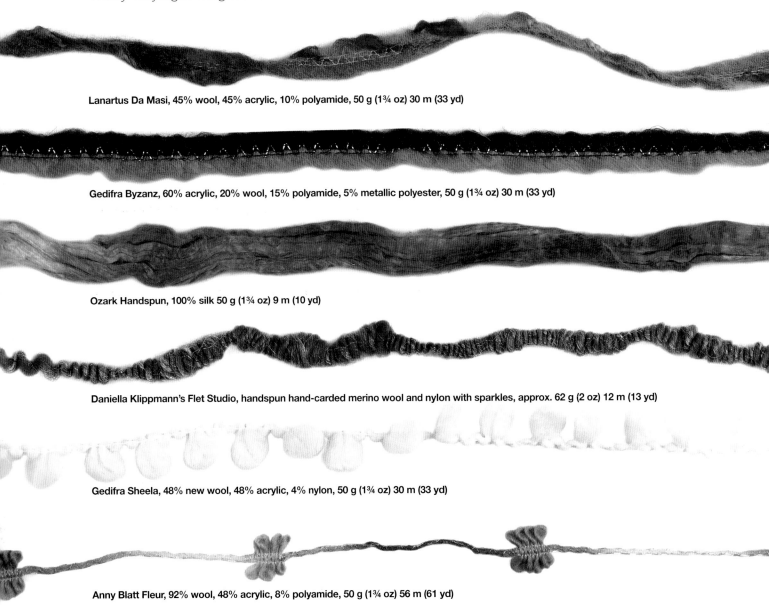

Lanartus Da Masi, 45% wool, 45% acrylic, 10% polyamide, 50 g (1¾ oz) 30 m (33 yd)

Gedifra Byzanz, 60% acrylic, 20% wool, 15% polyamide, 5% metallic polyester, 50 g (1¾ oz) 30 m (33 yd)

Ozark Handspun, 100% silk 50 g (1¾ oz) 9 m (10 yd)

Daniella Klippmann's Flet Studio, handspun hand-carded merino wool and nylon with sparkles, approx. 62 g (2 oz) 12 m (13 yd)

Gedifra Sheela, 48% new wool, 48% acrylic, 4% nylon, 50 g (1¾ oz) 30 m (33 yd)

Anny Blatt Fleur, 92% wool, 48% acrylic, 8% polyamide, 50 g (1¾ oz) 56 m (61 yd)

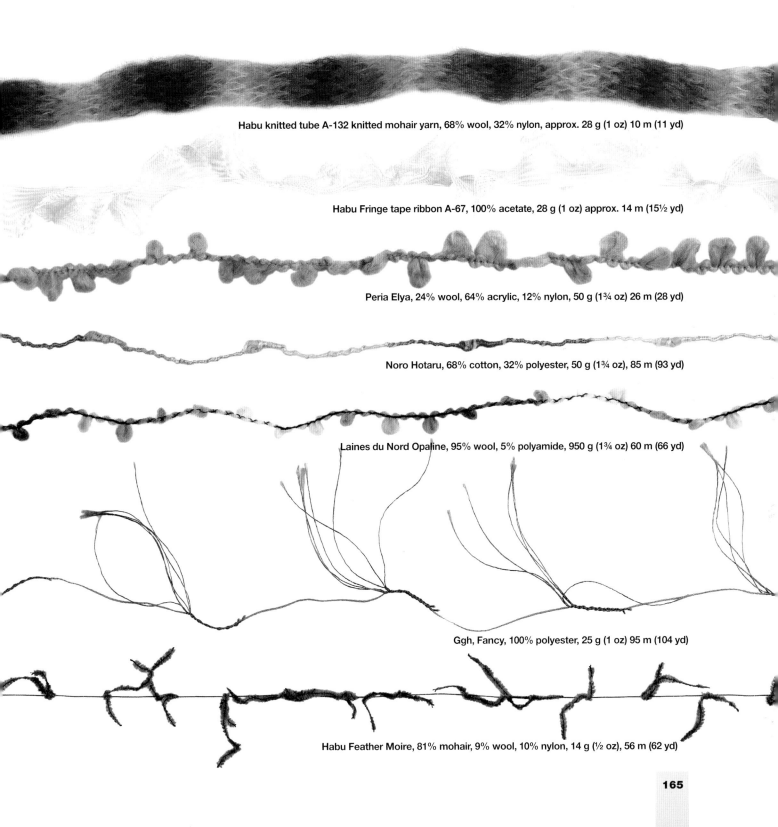

Habu knitted tube A-132 knitted mohair yarn, 68% wool, 32% nylon, approx. 28 g (1 oz) 10 m (11 yd)

Habu Fringe tape ribbon A-67, 100% acetate, 28 g (1 oz) approx. 14 m (15½ yd)

Peria Elya, 24% wool, 64% acrylic, 12% nylon, 50 g (1¾ oz) 26 m (28 yd)

Noro Hotaru, 68% cotton, 32% polyester, 50 g (1¾ oz), 85 m (93 yd)

Laines du Nord Opaline, 95% wool, 5% polyamide, 950 g (1¾ oz) 60 m (66 yd)

Ggh, Fancy, 100% polyester, 25 g (1 oz) 95 m (104 yd)

Habu Feather Moire, 81% mohair, 9% wool, 10% nylon, 14 g (½ oz), 56 m (62 yd)

Chunky

Chunky/bulky weight A much thicker yarn, used mainly for winter clothing, with a tension of about 12–15 sts to 10 cm (4 in).

Rowan Big Wool, 100% wool, 100 g (3½ oz) 80 m (87 yd)

Peria Puffy, 40% merino wool, 15% nylon, 45% acrylic, 50 g (1¾ oz) 45 m (49 yd)

Noro Iro, 75% wool, 25% silk yarn, 100 g (3½ oz) 120 m (131 yd)

Knitglobal Fleece, chunky bouclé, 64% ultrafine merino, 25% superfine kid mohair, 7% wool, 4% nylon, 100 g (3½ oz) 100 m (109 yd)

Knitglobal Shetland Flame, 96% wool, 4% nylon, 100 g (3½ oz) 100 m (109 yd)

Colinette Prism, 50% wool, 50% cotton, 100 g (3½ oz) 48 m (52 yd)

Colinette Grafitti, 100% wool, 100 g (3½ oz) 80 m (87½ yd)

Louisa Harding Silk Mountain, 63% wool, 25% silk, 12% kid mohair, 50 g (1¾ oz) 50 m (54½ yd)

Frog Tree chunky, 100% alpaca, 50 g (1¾ oz) 49 m (54 yd)

Debbie Bliss Cashmerino Chunky, 55% merino wool, 33% microfibre, 12% cashmere, 50 g (1¾ oz) 65 m (71 yd)

Frabjous Fibers, 100% Banana Silk Yarn, 200 g (7 oz) 145 m (159 yd)

Laceweight

2- or 3-ply/laceweight Extra-fine yarns, often mohair for lace knitting, the tension of these varies greatly.

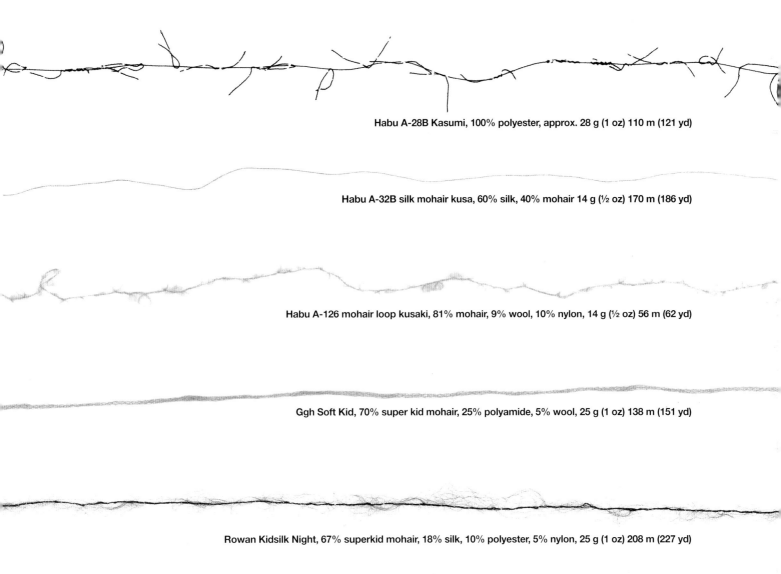

Habu A-28B Kasumi, 100% polyester, approx. 28 g (1 oz) 110 m (121 yd)

Habu A-32B silk mohair kusa, 60% silk, 40% mohair 14 g (½ oz) 170 m (186 yd)

Habu A-126 mohair loop kusaki, 81% mohair, 9% wool, 10% nylon, 14 g (½ oz) 56 m (62 yd)

Ggh Soft Kid, 70% super kid mohair, 25% polyamide, 5% wool, 25 g (1 oz) 138 m (151 yd)

Rowan Kidsilk Night, 67% superkid mohair, 18% silk, 10% polyester, 5% nylon, 25 g (1 oz) 208 m (227 yd)

Ribbon

Ribbon/fancy yarns Made from either strips of fabric or specially created ribbon, these have a variety of textures and weights. Most knit up on large- or small-gauge needles equally well.

Frabjous Fibers recycled sari ribbon, 10–20 mm (⅓–¾ in) wide, 50 g (1¾ oz) lengths vary

Louisa Harding Sari Ribbon, 90% polyamide, 10% metal, 50 g (1¾ oz) 30 m (33 yd)

Colinette Enigma, 55% cotton, 45% rayon, 100 g (3½ oz) 160 m (175 yd)

Colinette Tagliatelle, 90% wool, 45% rayon, 100 g (3½ oz) 145 m (139 yd)

Knit 1 Crochet 2 Tartelette, 50% cotton, 40% Tactel, 10% nylon, 50 g (1¾ oz) 70 m (76½ yd)

Colinette Giotto, 50% cotton, 40% rayon, 10% nylon, 100 g (3½ oz) 140 m (153 yd)

Colinette Wigwam, 100% cotton, 100 g (3½ oz) 130 m (142 yd)

Colinette Isis, 100% viscose, 100 g (3½ oz) 100 m (109 yd)

Colinette Mercury, 100% viscose, 50 g (1¾ oz) 62 m (68 yd)

Yarn Suppliers

These are the main contacts for the yarn used in this book, both small and large. Many thanks to them for sending the yarn that we used. Give them a call, or log on to their websites, to find a store near you.

In Europe

Adriafil
Selman's Creative Craft,
Unit 4, Townhead Mills
Main Street, Addingham
West Yorkshire LS29 0PD
01943 830034
www.adriafil.com

Daniela Kloppmann
Felt Studio
mail@feltstudio.co.uk
www.feltstudio.co.uk

Designer Yarns
Unit 8–10 Newbridge Industrial
Estate, Pitt Street, Keighley,
West Yorkshire
BD21 4PQ
01535 664222
www.designeryarns.uk.com

Get Knitted
39 Brislington Hill
Brislington, Bristol
BS4 5BE
0117 300 5211
www.getknitted.com

Ggh
Mühlenstraße 74
25421 Pinneberg
Germany
+49 (0) 4101 208484

Hawthorne Heritage Crafts
134 Wath Road,
Elsecar, South Yorkshire
S74 8JF
07801 949 108
hawthorneheritage.crafts@
yahoo.co.uk

The House of Hemp
Beeston Farm
Marhamchurch
Cornwall
EX23 0ET
01288 381638
www.thehouseofhemp.co.uk

Jamiesons Spinning Shetland
Sandness Industrial Estate
Sandness, Shetland, ZE2 9PL
01595 870 285
jamieson@zetnet.co.uk
www.jamiesonsshetland.co.uk

R.E. Dickie British Breed Yarns
West End Works
Parkinson Lane, Halifax
West Yorkshire, HX1 3UB
01422 341 516
www.dickie.co.uk

Scandinavian Knitting Design
Birgitte Eskebjerg Bailey
& Bruce Bailey
South Lodge, Wellington Court
Spencers Wood
Berkshire RG7 1BN
01189 884 226
www.scandinavianknittingdesign.com

The Woolly Shepherd
Val Grainger
Blagdon Hill, Somerset
01823 421 237
www.woollyshepherd.co.uk

In the US

Alchemy Yarn
PO Box 1080
Sebastopol, CA 95473
001 707 823 3276
www.alchemyyarns.com

Be Sweet
1315 Bridgeway,
Sausalito, CA 94965
001 415 331 9676
www.besweetproducts.com

Blue Sky Alpacas
PO Box 88
Cedar, MN 55011
001 763 753 5815
www.blueskyalpacas.com

Frabjous Fibers
5259 Augur Hole Road,
South Newfane VT 05351
www.recycledsilk.com/frabjous

Muench and Ggh Yarns
US Distributor: 1323 Scott Street
Petaluma, CA 94954-1135
001 707 763 9377
www.muenchyarns.com

Habu
135 West 29th Street
Suite 804 New York, NY 10001
001 212 239 3546
www.habutextiles.com

Jumbuk Distribution
Pear Tree Products
33941 Cape Cove
Dana Point, CA 92629
donnaandaus@aol.com

Kollage Yarns
3591 Cahaba Beach Road
Suite 101, Birmingham AL 35242
001 888 829 7758
001 205 408 5815
www.kollageyarns.com

Knitty Dirty Girl
Rachel Marie
Lancaster, PA
www.knittydirtygirl.com
artistrachelmarie@yahoo.com

Lorna's Laces Yarns
4229 N. Honore Street
Chicago, IL 60613
001 773 935 3803
www.lornaslaces.net

Shokay International
001 315 849 3319
US distributor:
anni@himalayayarn.com
001 802 862 6985
www.shokay.com

Tilli Tomas
72 Woodland Road
Jamaica Plain, MA 02130
001 617 524 3330
www.tillitomas.com

In Australia

Pear Tree Products
PO Box 463 Torquay
Victoria Australia 3228
+61 03 5261 6375
www.peartreeproducts.com.au
peartreeinfo@yahoo.com.au

Abbreviations

These are the most common abbreviations used. Special ones will be listed with each pattern.

alt	alternate	**cm**	centimetre(s)	**grp(s)**	group(s)
approx	approximately	**cn**	cable needle	**g st**	garter stitch
B	bobble	**CO**	cast on	**in.**	inch(es)
BC	back cross; back cable	**cont**	continue	**inc(s)**	increase(s), increasing
beg	beginning	**dc**	double crochet	**incl**	include, including
bet	between	**dec(s)**	decrease(s), decreasing	**K; k**	knit
BH	buttonhole	**DK**	double-knitting	**Kb; K1b**	knit stitch in row below, or knit stitch through back loop
BO	bind/cast off	**dpn**	double pointed needle(s)	**Kbf**	knit into back and front of same stitch
C	cable; cross	**est**	established	**Kfb**	knit into front and back of same stitch
CC	contrast colour	**FC**	front cross; front cable	**K2tog**	knit 2 together
ch	chain	**foll**	follow(ing)	**Kwise**	knitwise
col	colour	**g**	gram	**Kw2**	K1, wrapping yarn twice around needle

LC left cross; left cable
LH left hand
LHN left-hand needle
lp(s) loop(s)
LT left twist
M marker
m metre(s)
MB make bobble; bobble sizes vary between patterns
MC main colour

meas	measure(s)
mm	millimetre(s)
m1	make 1
m1k	make 1 by knitting into the back of the bar between stitches
m1tbl **or m1b**	make 1 through back loop; invisible increase
no.	number
oz	ounce
P; p	purl
patt	pattern
Pb; P1b	purl stitch in row below; or purl stitch through back loop
Pbf	purl into back and front of same stitch
Pfb	purl into front and back of same stitch
PM	place marker
pnso	pass next stitch over
psso	pass slip stitch over
Ptbl	purl through back loop
P2tog	purl 2 together
Pwise	purlwise
RC	right cross; right cable
rem	remaining
rep	repeat

rev st st	reverse stocking stitch
RH	right hand
RHN	right-hand needle
rib	ribbing
rnd(s)	round(s)
RS	right side (of work)
RT	right twist
sk	miss/skip
sl	slip
sl st	slip stitch
SM	slip marker
sp(s)	space(s)
ssk	slip, slip, knit
st(s)	stitch(es)
st st	stocking stitch
tbl	through back loop(s)
tch	turning chain
tog	together

tr	treble crochet
WS	wrong side (of work)
wyib	with yarn in back, as if to knit
wyif	with yarn in front, as if to purl
yb or ybk	yarn to the back between needles
yd	yard
yf or yfwd	yarn to the front between needles
yo or yon	yarn over needle to make extra stitch
yrn	yarn around needle to make extra stitch

Needle Conversions

These sizes are according to yarn standards. There are different size methods in most countries, so if in doubt, it may be best to rely on the metric sizes because these are an actual measurement.

Knitting needle sizes

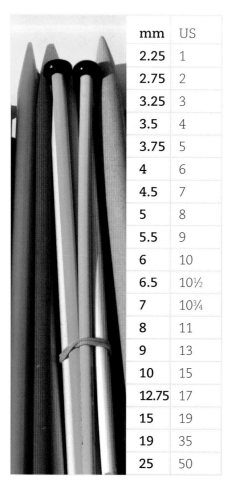

mm	US
2.25	1
2.75	2
3.25	3
3.5	4
3.75	5
4	6
4.5	7
5	8
5.5	9
6	10
6.5	10½
7	10¾
8	11
9	13
10	15
12.75	17
15	19
19	35
25	50

Crochet hook sizes

mm	US
2	
2.25	B-1
2.5	
2.75	C-2
3	
3.25	D-3
3.5	E-4
3.75	F-5
4	G-6
4.5	7
5	H-8
5.5	I-9
6	J-10
6.5	K-10
7	
8	L-11
9	M/N-13
10	N/P-15
12	
15	P/Q

Index

Acknowledgements

First, and most important, I must state that this book could not have come to fruition without the beautiful, unusual yarns currently being produced all around the world. My thanks to all those people and companies, small and large, who have contributed their wonderful fibres to *Knitter's Yarn Palette*. Special credit must go to those who spun bespoke yarn especially for the book: Daniela from felt studio and Debbie from Hawthorne Heritage Crafts. Thanks also to Fibrecrafts for lending the fibre samples for photography, and all the models who took part.

My gratitude is extended to Pauline, a fantastic knitter and friend, without whom I would not have been able to complete the book, and also to Linda, the most accomplished knitter I know! Thanks also to Julia, Sheila and Mhairi.

Thank you to Donna and all at Quintet who believed in the concept and have produced a beautiful book, and also to Katy, an extremely supportive, calm and encouraging editor, who has been there every step of the way with advice and brilliant proposals.

Finally, love and thanks as ever to Sean, who has to put up with tantrums at the most tense moments of my books.

Picture credits

a = *above*, b = *below*, l = *left*, r = *right*, c = *centre*

Alamy 32c–r, 32b–l, 33a–l, 47c, 48b–l, 74a, 76a–l, 76ac, 76c–r, 76b–l, 98a–l, 100b–l, 101a–l, 102c–l, 116a, 117a–r, 118a–l, 120a–r, 120c–l, 120b–l, 136a–l, 137a, 139a–l, 139b–r, 140b–l; **Corbis** 98b–r, **Getty** 20b, 22l, 30, 31a–c, 31a–r, 44b, 46c, 99a; **Shutterstock** 6, 10, 15r, 16b, 19a, 21a–r, 21b–r, 22c—r, 23 all, 27b, 31a–l, 31b–l, 32a–r, 32b–c, 32b–r, 33a–r, 33c–r, 33b–r, 34 all, 44a–l, 44a–r, 45a, 46a, 46b, 47a–l, 47b–l, 47b–r, 48c–l, 48b–r, 75a–l, 75a–r, 76a–r, 77a, 78c–l, 98a–r, 100a–l, 100c–l, 101a–r, 101c–r, 101b–r, 102a–l, 102b–l, 102b–r, 117b–l, 117c–r, 117b–r, 118c–r, 118a–r, 119a, 120a–l, 136b–l, 136b–c, 136b–r, 138c–l, 139a–r, 139b–l, 139c–r, 140a–r, 140b–r, 154

All other images are the copyright of Quintet Publishing ltd. While every effort has been made to credit contributors, Quintet Publishing would like to apologise should there have been any omissions or errors—and would be pleased to make the appropriate correction for future editions of the book.